ENDORSEMENTS

Restoring Broken Lives is an extremely interesting and motivational narrative about the birth and realization of a vision. Marion Spellman details the gut-wrenching personal family loss that led to the birth of Peniel Ministries. Struggling for years with limited resources, Marion's stalwart faith in God, personal fortitude, and the unwavering support of her husband, family, and friends have led to the restoration of hundreds of broken lives.

Today, Peniel Ministries is an exemplary rehabilitation ministry that is second to none and a testament to the faithfulness of God and the unflinching vision of one woman. I heartily endorse this book for all those who truly believe nothing is impossible with God.

—Dr. Kenneth R. Bell
Administrative Bishop of Pennsylvania
Church of God (Cleveland, Tennessee)

Restoring Broken Lives is a book that the world will be enriched by reading. Each page allows you to enter the joys, struggles, pains, and triumphs of the God-inspired and God-ordained ministry that has touched the lives of countless individuals. The writer's candor and unique presentation are a witness to the humility that has inspired such a magnificent journey. Very rarely are we blessed to experience such transparency. Each chapter allows us precious glimpses into the life of a yielded, yet very human vessel of the Lord.

This insightful collection of Dr. Spellman's experiences provides us with myriad examples of God at work in the affairs of His people. For those of us who are touched directly or indirectly by the power of addictive behavior, we are reminded of the redemptive power of Jesus Christ and His shed blood on Calvary. For any who are experiencing challenges in ministry, we receive encouragement to pursue the vision we have embraced. We are inspired to forge ahead, knowing we are empowered by the Holy Spirit. Readers facing adversity of any kind, minute or mammoth, are inspired to "keep it moving" after indulging this book.

One can only gain strength from this marvelous work. Only time and eternity will reveal the enormous impact that Dr. Spellman has had on the body of Christ and even the world, restoring "one broken life at a time." Her serious commitment to those who are bound by addiction is consistent with God's concern for those we may deem "the least of these." The story of Dr. Marion Spellman and Peniel Ministries is a contemporary memorial to the eternal existence of our omnipotent God and Savior. I am honored and humbled to call her my friend!

—Dr. Barbara M. Amos
Pastor Emeritus & Founding Pastor
Faith Deliverance Center (Norfolk, Virginia)

Restoring Broken Lives is proof-positive that no matter what the obstacles, all things are possible with God! The war on drugs is not going as advertised. The devastation of addiction—its cost on families and the soul of this nation—is staggering. Policy makers at the federal, state, and local levels throw money at this problem, while forgetting the principles upon which this nation was founded.

Every official dealing with the scourge of drug addiction should read this insightful, straightforward answer to an impossible task. This is a story of hope, an unlikely soldier, and a church of believers that wouldn't give up. The record of accomplishments at Peniel is unparalleled. I have personally witnessed the miracles that occur in this facility.

I am proud of Dr. Spellman and Peniel's allegiance to Johnstown and to this country.

—Bryan Barbin
State Representative
Johnstown, Pennsylvania

Everywhere you turn today, there is hopelessness. But there was a woman sent from God whose name was *Marion*. When she walks in, drug addiction walks out. When she walks in, depression walks out. When she walks in, low self-esteem walks out. When she walks in, strife walks out. When she walks in, the sick know help is on the way. She has heard the multitudes of pitiful, pleading voices and has been anointed to bring hope. Your life is never the same after Marion Spellman walks in.

This book will change the way you live, and the way you think. It is a manual for ministering to people. It shows you how to hear the voice of God. It shows you how to recognize the call of God for your life . . . how to build and operate a ministry . . . how to deal with staff relationships . . . how to develop a get-the-job-done attitude . . . how to handle rejection . . . how to deal with opposition . . . how to be a Proverbs 31 woman. When Marion heard those devastating words, "You have cancer," the fighting spirit kicked in again.

This was not a fight just for her life—it was a fight for drug-addicted men and women. But it was as if the Word of the Lord was saying, "Who are you, O great mountain? Before Marion, you shall become a plain . . . the hands of Marion have laid the foundation of this house; her hands shall also finish it." She fought, she won, and she is stronger than ever with a stronger anointing for helping people. This book is powerful and is a must-read for every Christian worker.

—Dr. Peggy Scarborough
Co-pastor of Socastee Church of God
Myrtle Beach, South Carolina

I am moved by the awe-inspiring vision of Dr. Marion Spellman. The transformation of lives I've personally witnessed through the years has unequivocally enhanced the body of Christ. It is evident that the power of deliverance through the shed blood of Jesus trumps the ploys and devices of Satan through the intense biblical curriculum required.

It is my prayer that the Spirit of the living God continues to flow mightily as rich seed is planted in the lives of each consumer!

—Pastor Carol Houston
Bethel Unspeakable Joy Church
Los Angeles, California

Transformation is defined as "a thorough or dramatic change." Peniel specializes in transformation. They use the Word of God and power of God to help you change.

Are you tired of living a life that is full of lying and deceit? Would you like to find victory over the demons that attack and haunt you? Peniel is not a place to learn behavior modification—it is a place to learn and experience true freedom.

I have ministered to hundreds of people who struggle with various addictions. Some places have little or no success, but Peniel is unequaled in its success. Your life is the sum of the choices you make, and you could not make a better choice than Peniel.

—Reverend Ray Streets
Emmanuel Baptist Church
Johnstown, Pennsylvania

When you walk in the front door of Peniel, the first thing you see is a sign that reads "At Last There's Hope"—hope to be free of addiction and live life God's way. He has made His wonderful works to be remembered.

Peniel was birthed in Dr. Spellman's heart when she was a young lady due to the addiction of her brother who later died of an overdose. From its small beginning to where it is today is nothing short of a miracle. The Peniel experience will give you help when you're hurting, hope when you're troubled, and answers to your questions to see the unmistakable hand of God.

—Betty Rice
Wife of Reverend Gene Rice
Former Chairman of Peniel Board of Directors

As a result of a divine encounter with God, Dr. Marion Spellman became unstoppable in what would be her calling in life. She began her journey of determining to provide a place of refuge for those who were bound by addictions and were living in a state of hopelessness.

It is one thing to say we have a burden for those who are bound and hurting. However, it is entirely different when that overwhelming desire is so intense that we take action and determine in our hearts to take the steps necessary to go forward in providing a place for help, restoration, and healing for those individuals. With qualified clinicians, Peniel is giving unconditional love, support, spiritual guidance, mentoring, and biblical teaching for people who have been caught in the trap of Satan's lies.

Because of Dr. Marion Spellman's response to the calling on her life, the success rate of Peniel is phenomenal with life-changing testimonies. Many have actually gone into full-time ministry. It is an honor to support a ministry like Peniel, especially when you have the awesome opportunity to visit the site that was born out of the heart of a willing vessel who was ready to meet the challenges that she would face, knowing she had the hand of God going before her, opening doors and moving obstacles to fulfill her dream.

This book will surely inspire and encourage many people who have a heart for ministry and will lead them to fulfill their call in the Kingdom.

—Jan Timmerman
Former Director of Church of God Women's Ministries
Cleveland, Tennessee

My acquaintance with Dr. Marion Spellman has been blessed as I have observed her life as she walks with God. Our acquaintance existed before she received the call of God to begin this great work for the kingdom of God.

Dr. Spellman has a burning desire to touch lives and point them to the Savior who can change their lives. Through our relationship the times have been difficult, but she maintained her faith and trust in God.

When I served as a member of Peniel's Board of Directors, I remember a time when we had no permanent home for the residents . . . and we had to move the entire operation at least five times. The faith that sustained the Spellmans revealed the guidance and direction for Peniel. I could see the hand of God at work.

Through those years when support and help came only from a few and many would not come on board, we observed Dr. Spellman as she pushed ahead through all the difficulties. I purposed in my heart to do what I could do to help her do this great work which God had called her to do.

Since the 1970s, we have witnessed the great things which God has done.

—Bishop J. Harold Palmer
Senior Pastor
Roxboro, North Carolina, Church of God

In a world rife with drug addiction, alcoholism, and abuse, Peniel Ministries gives the "outcasts of our society" a chance to get deliverance from dependence and return to society with transformed lives. Marion, chosen by God, has *penned* her compassion, motivation, and dedication to embrace this community in this book. As you read each chapter, you will see some of the struggles and disappointments she experienced trying to convince others to share her vision. Overall, Peniel has a phenomenal success rate.

I had the privilege of meeting Marion Spellman several years ago while serving on the International Women's Board of Directors for the Church of God. She presented Peniel Ministries to the board. Even though Peniel was not chosen as the World Missions project at that time, the board felt her compassion and encouraged her to follow her dream. Praise God, years later, the Women's Department accepted Peniel as its missions project, and today, the Church of God International Offices has Peniel as one of its ministries under the Care Division.

—Dorothy Sibley
International Women's Discipleship Advisory Committee
Wife of Assistant General Overseer Wallace J. Sibley
Church of God (Cleveland, Tennessee)

The first time I met Dr. Marion and Pastor Harold Spellman was when Peniel was operating in Somerset, Pennsylvania. From that time forward my husband, Robert, and I were in close contact as the ministry was continuing to develop.

When reading *Restoring Broken Lives*, it brought back memories of watching how our heavenly Father was in every step of the journey, and now there is a beautiful campus in Johnstown, Pennsylvania. It is a reminder of how God's timing works in everyone's life. She paints a vivid, yet humble self-portrait of a great leader. I am privileged to continue to be a part of her life and of Peniel Ministries.

Anyone who reads this book will be blessed and inspired by her testimony of how God leads and provides when we are willing to obey His calling.

—Mary Fisher
Wife of the late Dr. Robert Fisher
Former Chairman of Peniel Board of Directors

When I came to Peniel in 2004, my life had been broken and essentially destroyed by addiction. Actually, I thought I could never rise again in life or in the ministry. Dr. Spellman gave me a word from God: "You will preach again," she said firmly, "with more anointing, truth, and more power."

God did indeed give me back my life and my ministry just as Dr. Spellman declared to me in the name of the Lord. In fact, I was privileged to tell Marcus Lamb on Daystar's television network that Dr. Spellman was the most incredible woman I had ever met. God used her and Peniel Ministries to bring me back from the dead.

This book is a "must read" for every family in America and beyond, because it offers hope to those who appear to be hopeless.

—Bishop Ronald E. Brock
Proud Graduate of Peniel

Dr. Marion Spellman is one of those rare individuals who exemplifies servant leadership. Her heart exudes genuine love and care for those who have been incarcerated by drug/alcohol addiction. Her commitment to make a difference has been authenticated by academic preparation and practical engagement. Fulfilling her divine calling, she is founder and CEO of Peniel, a rehabilitation program that has witnessed the transformation of literally thousands of broken lives, both physically and spiritually. She is a dedicated Christian, a devoted wife and mother, and her life is a story that must be told. You will be inspired, stirred, and motivated by this book. Marion Spellman . . . inimitable, incomparable, irreplaceable—a choice servant of the Lord!

—Dr. Mike Baker
Administrative Bishop
Church of God in North Georgia

RESTORING BROKEN LIVES

The Marion Spellman Story

RESTORING BROKEN LIVES

The Marion Spellman Story

MARION SPELLMAN

WITH WANDA GRIFFITH

Unless otherwise noted, Scripture quotations are taken from the King James Version of the Bible.

Scripture quotations marked *NKJV* are taken from the *New King James Version*. Copyright© 1979, 1980, 1982, 1990, 1995, Thomas Nelson Inc., Publishers.

Editor: Wanda Griffith
Managing Editor of Publications: Lance Colkmire
Editorial Assistant: Tammy Hatfield
Copy Editor: Esther Metaxas
Cover Design: Michael McDonald
Technical Design: Gale Ard

ISBN: 978-1-59684-819-1

Visit *www.pathwaypress.org* for more information.

Printed in the United States of America

DEDICATION

This book is dedicated to my beloved father, Ivrie Pegues Sr., and to my incredible mother, Margaret Minnie Bridges. Their perseverance and example set the foundation for my choices in this lifelong journey.

To the memory of my brother, Ivrie "Puddin" Pegues Jr., whom I will always dearly love. To this day, it breaks my heart to know he died alone of a drug overdose in Oakland, California, on September 18, 1993.

To our son, Skip, and his beautiful family. Throughout his childhood, Skip endured the challenges of this journey with us. He was there, steady as a rock, on the mountaintops as well as in the valleys. To me, Skip is a true champion.

And to my baby sister, Lori Curry, whom I deeply love and admire, as well as to her family. Lori has been a tremendous help and a great inspiration to me while writing this book. She was always available to help. Lori does not seek applause; she is busy looking for another opportunity to serve.

And finally, to my beloved husband, Harold "Spelly" Spellman, who is always there in the midnight hours, ready to encourage, to shield, and to protect me—even from myself. I cannot imagine my life without him.

ACKNOWLEDGMENTS

I wish to acknowledge Wanda Griffith, who spent many hours editing this manuscript and had the patience to work with a novice writer. She realized it was important to me that I express the journey of Peniel in my own words. For several years, Wanda's passion and encouragement for me to tell the Peniel story is the reason this book has become a reality.

Also, I would like to sincerely thank the Peniel team for praying for me as I wrote this book. Their support was beyond measure. But that's who they are, and that's what they do. The Peniel team is awesome!

TABLE OF CONTENTS

FOREWORD

I consider it an incredible honor to not only serve on Dr. Marion Spellman's board of directors for the Peniel Residential Treatment Center but also to have become her friend. Having known of her for many years and admiring her from afar, I never dreamed the Lord would bless me with the privilege to share her burden and contribute in my small way to her powerful ministry.

My first introduction to Peniel was during the Pennsylvania Church of God Camp Meeting in Somerset in July 1991. My husband, then known as Evangelist Mark L. Williams, was the night speaker, and the Peniel Choir ministered in music. It was an open-air tabernacle, and those men rocked the walls and metal roof with their hand-clapping, foot-stomping, full-voice singing and their uninhibited Pentecostal style of worship. Mark loved ministering to them because they were so responsive and worshiped in the Word with such exuberance, which made his preaching a joy, not a labor. What an impression they made on me! Those who had been forgiven much had much to give in worship to their Lord. It was a beautiful expression of hope and grace.

During an evening service of the camp meeting, as usual the altars were filled. Among them was Bill Henry, a student in the Peniel program. He eagerly responded to my husband's message and was gloriously saved that night. After graduating from the program, Bill married Susan, Dr. Spellman's secretary. Bill went back to college, received his counseling credentials, and is now a primary counselor at Peniel and a senior elder in the Peniel Praise Community Church.

I stood in awe that Marion Spellman, a woman, was leading all of those robust men to freedom in Christ. In my young mind, I thought, She must be really smart, strong, and spiritually mighty. Quite frankly, she intimidated me. Little did I know that our paths would cross years later.

I will never forget the International Women's Banquet of the Church of God General Assembly on Thursday, August 5, 2004, in San Antonio, Texas. Peniel had been selected for the Women With A Mission (WWAM) project for that two-year period of fund-raising. I was serving in Fresno as the regional Women's Ministry president for California/Nevada. For years I had attended these biannual banquets, where everyone wore their finest clothes in hopes of hearing their name called for an award of some sort. These events were lengthy. We would sit there while pictures were being made of winning groups, leaders bragging on each other, servers scrambling, and dishes clattering until the last award and "thank you" was given. However, that year's event was different!

The obvious anointing of God was in that ballroom as much as any worship service I had attended. Why? Because Dr. Marion Spellman and her group from Peniel ministered in song with the same passion I had seen years before at that camp meeting in Pennsylvania. The Spirit of the Lord moved, and women were weeping and worshiping.

Harold Ashlock, a Texan, was there to boldly, yet humbly, testify of his son's recovery and rehabilitation at Peniel. Other clients shared their stories of redemption that gripped our hearts with the vision to see bondages broken in our circles of influence. There was not a dry eye in the room. This made us acknowledge the problem was not just on the streets or in the schools, but right inside our own churches—indeed within our own families.

We were not sending money overseas to an orphanage, or building an educational facility around the world that we would never see. We were raising money to help our own sons and daughters of the church to break the power of addiction with the proven power of Almighty God. This serious social decay was creeping too close to home.

The following year, in August 2005, Marion invited all the Church of God women's ministries presidents who had been raising funds to attend the Peniel graduation. Many bishops and their wives gathered to see what Peniel was all about. Because our boys were small and we had no family in California, I left them with their dad and flew to Pittsburgh, rented a car, and headed to the graduation weekend of events in Johnstown.

Marion and her husband, Bishop Harold Spellman, were the perfect hosts. Their excitement was contagious. You could tell the staff and clients were pumped. Not expecting her to remember me or know who I was, I wanted to introduce myself to Marion, thank her for the invitation, and express my support. She embraced me warmly, complimented me, and thanked me for coming. Wow! Maybe she was not as intimidating as I had previously thought.

Throughout the weekend, we heard testimonies from clients of all ages and backgrounds—young mothers who were torn from their children, young men who were incarcerated in their teens, married men who had lost their families, and one older guy whose eighty-plus-year-old mother was there to see him graduate free from the bondage of drugs. Tissues were in great demand at every event—the banquet, the graduation service, and the Sunday morning celebration.

We heard alumni who were now leading successful lives share about their years of freedom and ministry since graduating. Spouses and children were reuniting with their families because of their unique Peniel experience. I thought of relatives, friends, and church members who needed the hope Peniel offers. I was hooked! I made a promise to Marion that even after the WWAM project ended, I would be a supporter both in prayer and finance to this life-changing, hope-giving, healing/deliverance ministry.

Addiction. What an ugly word—one that the church certainly wasn't ready to address in the 1970s! However, one courageous woman was ready and willing to answer the call. Today, few families escape the painful claws of addiction, whether it is through alcohol, drugs, pornography, gambling, sex, food, or some other controlling issue. My husband has preached too many funerals because of alcohol and drugs. Too many marriages, families, and ministries have been destroyed because of addictions. Yet, we live in a society where recreational drinking, drug use, and smoking marijuana are accepted and even endorsed by those in the government. We can close our eyes like the church of yesteryear, or we can face this demon head-on with our only hope—Jesus Christ. Read Marion's story and see how it's done.

This book chronicles Marion's journey, starting with her call from God through life's crooked course, and finally the culmination of founding and directing Peniel. If God could use a single black mother in a day of racial prejudice and persecution to answer His call, imagine what He could do through you.

Dr. Marion Spellman has faced heartaches and hallelujahs, betrayals and blessings, sorrows and smiles, life-threatening physical trials and miraculous triumphs—and she has come out victorious, giving glory to her God. What a woman! What a story! Read on and be inspired.

—Sandra Kay Williams
Wife of General Overseer Mark L. Williams
Church of God International Women's Director
Cleveland, Tennessee

INTRODUCTION

Except for occasional flashes of headlights coming through the window, the room was exceptionally dark and the silence was almost frightening. In the stillness of the night, I felt a supernatural presence of the Holy Spirit. Like Jacob in Genesis 32, I was about to experience a divine visitation—a face-to-face encounter with Almighty God.

As tears of conviction flowed down my cheeks, I could hear deep within my spirit the cries of helpless individuals entangled in the addictive web of alcohol and drug abuse. Their hopeless words rang out: "Once an addict, always an addict. If we go here or there . . . still, we will surely die."

I discerned something supernatural was happening to me—I was in the midst of a heavenly visitation. I had read about these kinds of occurrences in Scripture, but they were rare and certainly only happened to exceptional people. How could an ordinary person like me have a personal encounter with the awesome living God?

Like all of those before me, my legs would not support me. I fell to the floor and lay reverently prostrate before Him. Softly and uncontrollably, I wept. I cannot tell you when my weeping turned into a soul-wrenching lament, but from the depths of my being, I felt an incredible pain—a spirit of mourning—and I knew this time with the Lord would be indelibly etched on my heart.

Why was I in such distress? I could not interpret what it all meant or how I should respond. One thing I knew for sure: God was in the house, and He came to speak with me personally.

Eventually, I could hear muffled voices, but I could not understand what they were saying. Gradually, the voices became pitiful, pleading voices crying out in distress. There were multitudes, yet each one stood alone. The scene took my breath away and broke my heart. Blinding tears were now flooding my face, staining my blouse, and settling in small puddles before me.

The empty Kleenex box and crumpled piles of wet tissues symbolized the pain and emotions of the moment . . . but my weeping was not enough to compensate for the pain and cries of the helpless multitude. I could see the desperation of those entangled in the relentless web of addiction. I saw children in the drizzling rain with tear-stained faces. I revisited the pain and hopelessness that my own mother experienced when she heard her only son had been beaten by the police and incarcerated for a drug-related crime. Right then, I determined I would do whatever it took to dry my mother's tears and change my brother's life.

God opened my eyes also to see the gaunt faces of throwaway children who were abused, hungry, and forgotten. One by one their cries rang out, "I'm afraid and I'm lost." Then He said to me, "The people I have shown you are bound. They are bound because of what they believe! But there is nothing impossible with God. I have power over all sin. You have been chosen to show them another way—a better way."

I realized the people in my vision had bought the big lie that drug and alcohol dependency is permanent and the very thought of deliverance is a hopeless dream. Their mantra sadly declared, "Once addicted, always addicted!"

O my God, I thought. *Look at the incredible potential in their faces.* They came from every class and every nation. They were weak and sickly, and they were marching unknowingly toward eternal destruction. Somehow, I knew the root of their problems was spiritual.

Suddenly, as my eyes met with these broken people, I realized we were making a supernatural connection. We began communicating nonverbally. They were expecting me to answer their questions and provide them with solutions. I felt overwhelmed.

As I tried to figure out an answer, the scene expanded to include more people—mothers, fathers, and even newborn babies bound by drugs. Then there were the drug dealers, criminals driven by their addiction who had committed horrendous deeds, and still others. Massive groups of addicted people appeared.

Burying my head in my hands, I cried aloud, "Stop it! What can I do? What do You want?" With that cry, I knew this was my "burning-bush" experience, but it was too difficult for me to endure. Dramatically, God was awakening something miraculous within my heart—something I would find impossible to explain to my family and friends.

The memory of this night would take me through the lean, lonely years ahead. Just the thought of this frightening yet marvelous time with God would arouse me in the middle of the night and cause me to seek His face. Indeed, I would have many more times with Him—some I will never share. These times would energize me in the coming days, especially when I felt my strength was depleted. He was anointing me for the special ministry of Peniel—a ministry of restoring broken lives that would both rescue the perishing and care for the dying. This anointing was for a special ministry born in the heart of Almighty God.

When I think about it, I guess I always knew God was calling me for something, and this experience was a confirmation that would guide my destiny.

My first sign that God had repositioned me was on a day I drove across town to take my mother to lunch. I was on a mission to comfort her. If one of her children was in trouble, it meant that she—the woman who "wrote the book" on good mothering—was also in trouble.

My brother, "Puddin," a member of the U.S. Air Force, had returned from Vietnam addicted to drugs. He spent years trying to fight the drug demon, but to no avail. Police had beaten him so badly that he was unrecognizable. They arrested him on drug-related charges, and my mother had slumped into a deep state of depression, confusion, and despair.

I prayed for direction and words of comfort as I drove to my assignment. Slowly coasting into a parking space, I nervously pondered what I would say to the dearest person in the world to me. I was determined to do whatever it took to dry my mother's tears and rescue my only brother.

What will it take, I wondered, *to break the relentless grip of a habit so strong that entangled a young, handsome, intelligent man, who was full of promise? How could he break free of the dangerous subculture that accompanies addiction*? Yes, it would demand more than a personal resolution. What could I do, or where should I begin? I didn't have a clue, but the more I prayed for God to lift this crushing burden, the heavier it became in my heart. Yes, I believe God was calling me to a special ministry, and He would begin it first in "Jerusalem"—my own family.

Like Moses, I had my share of excuses:

"Lord, the economy is poor. The resources are so limited."

"Many believe that even the born-again experience is not enough to free a person addicted to drugs and alcohol. What could I do to change the course of an international epidemic that had baffled some of the world's greatest minds?"

"Lord, will they really believe that You have sent me?"

Then there were my own unspoken issues, which were my constant companions. I am a *woman*—a *black woman*. Painful high-school memories of both subtle and blatant discrimination haunted me. I feared what my response would be if I had to relive those agonizing years again. Would bitterness enter my heart, jeopardizing my intimate relationship with God? In time, God and I would work through all of that with a plan I continue to use to this day.

After all my excuses were exhausted, a great peace settled over me. A quiet confidence replaced all my doubts and fears. Instead, I was filled with joy and gratitude. I recognized that I was indeed a blessed woman, with the honor of being called to serve the living God on a specific assignment. I had been selected! I could hear the gentle voice of the Master: *Look up! Fix your eyes on the Son. I will grant your petitions if you will obey Me.*

In obedience, I accepted His hand of grace as He spoke peace to me through His Word: "Call unto me, and I will answer thee, and shew thee great and mighty things" (Jer. 33:3). My calling and election was sure. I was falling in love with the "lepers" of society. I wanted quality time with the drug addict. I wanted to tenderly hold that child whose mother was somewhere high and unconcerned.

I left my divine encounter not with a limp like Jacob, but with a burning passion that would accompany my husband-to-be, Harold Spellman, and me for the rest of our lives. We would call the place *Peniel*—the place where men and women would meet God face-to-face, and He would preserve their lives (see Gen. 32:30).

CHAPTER 1

FAMILY LIFE: FOUNDATIONAL BUILDING BLOCKS

Long gone are the fenced-in porches, manicured lawns, and tree-lined streets where children play safely and enjoy a healthy, uninterrupted childhood. Today the symbols of comfort and safety have been replaced with armed police, metal detectors in schools, and aggressive anti-bullying signs. The fallout from sin is devastating. We are desperate for biblical truth and a face-to-face encounter with Almighty God. Indeed, boldly presenting the gospel is humanity's only answer for guiding a lost generation toward a hope-filled and secure future. We must take this gospel to our dying generation and convince them of a better way to invest their shattered lives.

My Early Years

My preschool years were in the small town of Rankin, Pennsylvania, and later we moved to Swissvale, about thirty miles away. I cannot remember our town making headline news about anything. Still, the hustle and bustle of trying to make a living was obvious and common for us and our neighbors. Similar economic and social challenges were shared by all.

I want to introduce you to my family. Daddy only had a fourth-grade education, but he was very loyal to his job with an enviable work ethic. He labored long hours in the local steel mill. I remember waking up and hearing him leave early in the morning while it was still dark. It was in the mills that both of his legs were severely burned when hot liquid steel was inadvertently spilled on him. Because he was uninformed, he was never compensated for this accident. This injury plagued him for the rest of his life, and I believe that it ultimately contributed to his death.

My dad was a strong and loving influence in my life. I absolutely adored him, even though I found out in my adult years that he was a bit of a rascal. He was very handsome and all the ladies liked him a lot! The problem was, he liked them back. I always felt that deep inside he was ashamed because he did not have the opportunity for the education he desired. Perhaps the admiration of women met an emotional need and he compensated by becoming a local Casanova.

Daddy
(Irvin Pegues Sr.)

Daddy would not miss a day of work, but he was a gambler. It was anyone's guess what time he would arrive home on payday! We would all laugh as my mother told the same story, over and over. When she asked Daddy what happened to his paycheck, he said a strong wind just came and blew it right out of his shirt pocket. He told that same outrageous story so many times that he started to believe it himself . . . and he wanted Momma to believe it too.

He also was a weekend drinker. Ah, Daddy! Now that I think about it, he was probably a good candidate for Peniel. As ridiculous as it sounds—and you may not believe this—my father loved his family dearly. My mother proclaimed this truth until she died—you just had to know him! He lacked living skills that would help him to make difficult decisions. He was a child laborer in the fields of South Carolina, where he also spent his youth. He was not afforded educational privileges, so, as my husband would say, "He did the best he could with what he had to work with."

On the other hand, Momma's routine was completely predictable. She would make us breakfast, clean us up, and allow us to play on the screened-in porch. She would leave the front door and windows open so she was able to hear and see her children as she went about her daily chores.

"Momma! Tell Baby to stop saying hi to everybody that passes by," my annoyed brother, "Puddin," would say, referring to me by his special nickname. "They are not even saying hi back to her."

I can still hear Momma's stern warning to us as we squabbled on the porch: "Baby, don't be so bossy . . . and Puddin, please . . . stop teasing your sister." We did not know it at the time, but Momma was subtly introducing us to the "Pegues Family No-Fighting Code." She was the author and finisher of this non-negotiable Pegues behavior requirement, which was destined to transcend many generations.

My parents named me Marion Mattie after my father's mother, whose name was Mattie Marion, but my brother could not pronounce my name, so he just called me "Baby." This family nickname remains with me to this day.

"Puddin"
(Irvin Pegues Jr.—Brother)

My only brother, Ivrie Pegues Jr., was also my best friend. He was awesome in my sight, and he loved and protected his little sister. Everyone called him "Puddin." I don't know how and when he got this nickname, but I know it came directly out of my Mother's heart.

Momma's Nicknames

Momma definitely encouraged the nicknames, which became a family tradition that my sister and I have continued to this day. Momma made nicknames a common and endearing family custom. She would make up names for everything! She was so creative, and it was so much fun to hear what she would come up with next. When we were very good, she would call us her "cute 'n' nice."

When she wanted us to eat something we didn't like, she would name that meal "the goodie ole stuff-stuff dish." She knew how to entice us to eat. She would appear distracted because she was overcome with her exciting song and her self-identified scrumptious food that we had already said we didn't like. It was always the same words and tune. My son, Skipper, knows it and could sing it for you right now! In fact, some of my sons and daughters in the Lord know the "Goodie Ole Stuff-Stuff" song. It was such a catchy song and Momma had a ball singing it. I could never remember just which verse it was that I would find myself singing, devouring and enjoying that goodie ole stuff-stuff, which I had vowed I would never eat, but this scene always ended the same!

So many times she would have us in stitches laughing at her descriptions of something she didn't like. She would say, "That outfit is lookin' like a door facin'." To this day, I have never discovered exactly what a door facin' is.

When Momma was serving one of our favorite desserts—and we kids just couldn't wait to be served our portion—she would often express her great love for her children. "You are so special, and this stuff-stuff is just for you," she would say as she smiled and filled our plates.

I don't know how long my mother and father were married before they separated and finally divorced. It was a subject we didn't talk about. After the breakup, we lived with my mother, and she made an obvious effort to shield us from family problems. Both she and my dad always assured us that what happened between them had absolutely nothing to do with us. So we grew up with a deep and committed love for both of our parents.

Meet "Pamper"

After Puddin and I somewhat healed from the family breakup, my mother met and fell in love with a wonderful man named Irvin Bridges (nicknamed "Pamper"), who had a unique personality. I can see why Momma married him. He prided himself as being a self-made man. He loved and treated Puddin and me as if we were his own children. My earliest memories of him involved the wonderful earthy smell of his Old Spice cologne. I loved greeting him with a big hug. He always smelled so good!

"Pamper"
(Irvin Bridges)

Pamper was from an era that dressed to impress. I would describe him as having a James Cagney persona minus the criminal element. He was a hardworking "Joe" that made his mark in the industrial age of America's history. He, too, was a steel-mill worker who eventually became a bricklayer foreman. This was a position and title he wore with great pride. It was not easy for black men to obtain promotions of any kind in those days, yet he was able to achieve a commendable level of respect among the administration. Because of his employment achievements, he even acquired a level of status and recognition in his community and specifically among his peers.

Ah, the neighborhood where legends were made and how-to stories were shared. Middle America was booming and we were on the brink of the technological age. He was proud to work long hours, make a decent living, and even purchase a brand-new car every few years. He would choose Buick 225 and Cadillac models; no other brands would do. That was a sure sign of success for a man with limited education. Pamper had uncanny common sense, street savvy, and an extraordinary work ethic.

My Sister

When I was in junior high school, Pamper and Momma presented the family with our baby sister. She was so cute and smart as a whip. Little Lori was an unexpected gift from God. We also had a nickname for her, but by now, you probably knew that! What you probably didn't guess is I am the one who gave her this name. From the beginning, I called her "Lo." (I guess I subconsciously wanted to beat Momma to the punch!)

Puddin and I embraced Lori and taught her the no-fighting-among-siblings code. Its goal was to maintain a close-knit family. Still, this was much easier said than done because we would often challenge the code's strength. Lo and I went through a time of great testing. We had a misunderstanding that was so devastating it caused a serious breach in our relationship that lasted several years. We were cordial to each other, but you could freeze a popsicle in the room when we were together. If there was any conversation at all, it was always directed to the neutral person in the room. Not to worry, one of us would surely be making our exit momentarily; the room was not big enough for both of us.

My husband, Harold ("Spelly"), would have no part in what he labeled as "downright foolishness." The Lord knows he spent hours encouraging me to forgive, repent, and let go, but I just couldn't move on. I was stuck.

Strangely enough, I did not even think about Lori or the hostility between us until I would see her. Spelly would tell me this was what frightened him most. "The devil is deceiving you," he would warn. "Because you don't normally think about this sin, does not mean God has also forgotten it. Suppose you die without thinking about Lori. Do you think this sin you are fully aware of will simply be overlooked?"

I wish that I could say something spiritual, like I was immediately able to overcome our differences through consecrated prayer. After all, she is my baby sister and she was not even saved at that time, but I am ashamed to admit this was not the case.

Momma was uncharacteristically silent on the matter. How disturbing was that? I did notice, however, that she had something secretly going on with God. Then one day I saw it . . . I had seen it before! I saw something that I had begged God to never be able to see in my mother's eyes again. She was silently weeping! She seemed to be in such pain, and even though I was in the room, she was all alone. The tears puddled under her chin.

"Momma, what is it? What in the world is wrong?"

"This thing between you and your sister is against everything I taught you!" she said. "You are the oldest, and the greater responsibility is yours. Don't let me leave this world with you girls in this condition—please!"

"You won't, Momma, I promise!" It was now clear to me—I understood who the true enemy was. I told my husband I was ready to release this albatross that had been oppressing me.

"Yes, Babe," he said. "Yes, we are ready to claim our victory and to reclaim our sister." We prayed together, and God broke that unforgiving diabolical spirit in my life. Days later, my beloved baby sister and her husband, Andre, received Christ as their Savior and have never looked back. They are leaders in our church, and Lori has spent many hours helping me to pull the manuscript for this book together.

To this day, we do not argue with each other. The no-fighting code still serves its purpose. We will discuss a matter and respect the other's opinion, but we will never go beyond that invisible boundary.

Both Puddin and Lori far exceeded me in academics. For me, good grades required studying like a house on fire. Meanwhile, my brother could practically memorize a book in one sitting. He rarely had to study, and still passed with high marks. And incredible Lori had the spontaneous wit of Carol Burnett and the intellect of a scholar. When I would complain to Momma about how hard it was for me to learn and how easy it was for my siblings, she would smile and say, "Well, Honey, you are just my 'slow' child." We would all "crack up" laughing. Then she would become serious and say, "Everyone has his or her own gifts, and Baby, know that you have gifts of great value." Thank God, I had the nerve to believe her!

"Lo"
(Lori Curry—Sister)

Momma's Second Wind

My mother was the greatest woman I have ever known. She ranks at the top of my "most-admired and loved" list. During our school years, she worked long, hard hours cleaning houses during the day and going to beauty-culture school at night. Aunt Sis, who was my mother's only sister, with six children of her own, watched my brother and me while Momma worked.

In spite of overwhelming odds and facing an uncertain future with two young children, Momma was able to get her "second wind," and became a successful businessperson. She was black, she was a woman, and she was divorced; yet, she became the owner of her own beauty salon in a nice section of town. She was able to hire two beauticians to work in her shop. She accomplished this at a time when racism was flourishing and opportunities for someone in her situation were almost nonexistent.

However, no one told my mother that what she was doing could not be done, so she continued her quest for a better life by furthering her educational goals. She later enrolled in college and studied nursing, but because she was the oldest in her class, the younger students were often unkind. Still, she persevered to become a licensed practical nurse and later a registered nurse. Her long-term plans were to return to school and earn her doctorate. I am convinced she would have achieved that goal . . . except her health began to fail.

"NeeNee"
(Mom Bridges)

The Care-Giving Years

Spelly and I had the privilege of ministering first to my dad and then to my mother in our home during their latter years and in the time of their illnesses. We considered it our great and cherished privilege to build and decorate a special room that was medically equipped for their individual care. After a long and undignified illness, Daddy peacefully died of multiple sclerosis with my husband at his side reading him Scripture, as he ushered him into the waiting and loving arms of our Savior. We had the wonderful opportunity to lead him to the Lord before he died.

Many years later, we had the same privilege of bringing my mother into our home. We witnessed her courageous fight against Parkinson's disease. Through her suffering, Momma amazed the doctors and friends with her resilient, unshakable commitment to God. For months, she came so close to leaving us, only to keep bouncing back. Dr. Gene Rice, chairman of the Peniel Board at that time, and his wife, Betty, had promised to officiate at her home-going celebration, which came at a most unlikely time. On the third day of a Peniel graduation weekend, during the early hours of Sunday, Momma was summoned to the ultimate commencement celebration in the sky.

Whew! What a difficult time! At times, I can still feel the pain and struggle of releasing her and find myself wishing I had done more for her because she deserved so much more. I was never able to accept the fact she was ill and aging. I wanted to keep her vibrant and young as she was during my formative years, but she graduated to a higher calling. My mother knew how to live, and she definitely knew how to die. Everything she did, she did with dignity and distinction. She just went to sleep . . . and she was not!

At the end of each chapter, you will find the testimony of someone whose life has been transformed through Peniel.

A Walking Miracle

I was blinded by drug-and-alcohol addiction. From an early age, the cycle began to emerge: leaving home, lying, cheating, stealing, flunking classes, and misbehaving. I began experimenting with alcohol at the age of thirteen, and by the time I was a freshman in high school I used illegal substances every day.

After school one Tuesday in my senior year, I was surprised when my father met me at a time that I would normally get high. He took me to a place called *Peniel* and told me I had a counseling session. I went to counseling for the remainder of my senior year. Peniel helped me to graduate high school and get accepted to Saint Francis University, but I instead decided to continue using drugs and alcohol.

For another year and a half, I continued on my downward spiral that led me to a point to where I looked up and saw the Lord. I opened the Bible and began reading in Genesis. When I got to chapter 32, I read about Jacob's encounter at a place called *Peniel*.

So, I checked into Peniel's treatment program a short time after and spent thirteen rigorous months learning how to live a happy, healthy, and sober lifestyle. I began my university education during my inpatient drug-and-alcohol treatment with Peniel's pilot online degree program, in which I completed two English composition courses. By the time I completed inpatient treatment, I enrolled in a branch campus of the University of Pittsburgh. Upon completion of my undergraduate degree, I intend to study international law in the United Kingdom.

The success I have achieved in my educational endeavors makes me proud, but it is not the source of my satisfaction. The source of my joy comes from the improbability of my success and the inner knowledge I am a walking miracle.—*Joshua (Pennsylvania)*

CHAPTER 2

PUTTING AWAY CHILDISH THINGS

We grew up when equal rights was only a dream, and racism was prominent. It was difficult for us to imagine ourselves ever heading companies or rising above the status quo; yet, there were occasional signs of a better world. It was natural to follow the path that was charted by our parents before us. Earning enough money was always an issue, and strong family values remained a primary virtue.

The era I was raised in was one of family-oriented life. Parents worked, and the family structure centered on the home and the church. My grandfather was a senior trustee in the Union Baptist Church in Swissvale, Pennsylvania. This was a prestigious position in the religious community. I was brought up to be God-conscious, but my family did not know the Lord as Savior. As a child in school, I loved to write poems that always seemed to be God-centered. Indeed, as a child, God was vying for my attention and for my allegiance; I just didn't know it.

While in high school, I was asked by one of my teachers to write a poem for our Christmas celebration. I was unsaved, but I knew the story of the birth of Christ, so I could do that! No problem.

Christmas bells are daily ringing;
Shoppers rushing, choirs singing.
Children hoping with all their might
Santa won't pass their home tonight.

A few think of the wonderful sight
When Christ was born by mere starlight.
And when the Wise Men brought to Him
Gifts within the manger dim.

A King who was born to do good deeds
To every nation, color, and creed;
A King who gave us freedom to live
To love, to work, to pray, to give.

And on this day—this Christmas season
Give God some time for one big reason
Because He gave us without a doubt
Blessings we could never count.

And on His birthday take time to say,
"Good morning, dear God and Happy Birthday."
And He in turn will smile at you
And think it wasn't so hard to do.

I could never be accused of being reluctant. Some people say I was born with an abundant amount of determination and a spirit of "Go for it!" Nothing could stop me from taking a leap of faith, because I have only one gear—overdrive! This trait would prove to be an asset that would be a driving force throughout the ministry.

I am confident that this drive came from my mother. She tells the story of my hospitalization at the age of two years old. I was bed-ridden for months with pneumonia that developed into a life-threatening situation.

According to Momma, the doctors had given me a spinal tap without her permission or knowledge. The doctor left specific orders that I lie flat on my back for several hours—except no one told Momma. When she came in later that morning to visit me, she picked me up to comfort me and to play with me as she always did. Because she moved me prematurely, they told her I would never walk again. But Momma would not receive their report. She worked daily for hours, massaging my joints and encouraging me to take small steps . . . and then larger ones, until my muscles and joints became strong. I could walk when she brought me in that hospital, and she meant for me to walk after I came home. End of story!

An Abusive Marriage

As I ventured into an ill-advised marriage, I gained a formal education that only "living it out" can provide. As a naive eighteen-year-old, I was thrust into a shocking and challenging life. Some of the pain was because of choices and responses I made, and some of the agony was the result of my husband's abusive patterns that created an intense sense of trembling and fear within me. I learned difficult, but valuable, lessons that molded my life.

Today we live in a disposable world where relationships as well as life-lessons are not given the opportunity to grow and mature us. However, I was taught to work it out and stick it out. Momma's favorite saying was, "When the road gets tough, the tough get going." Although my first husband died, I used my pain to motivate me to minister to hurting men and women. I had not realized God always has a way of escape; then, I only knew I needed to survive.

During those early days, I was a single parent responsible for a young son and a very sick father. I remember giving my mother the woe-is-me speech. She tenderly listened to me, nodding her head in all the right places. Then she spoke: "Honey, I did my job when I raised you kids. I am too old and too tired to raise yours. Now you are not the only single parent in this world, so this is not strange. Women around the world are doing what you have been asked to do, and you can do this! You have what it takes to do this." And . . . I did it!

Defining Moments

I began attending the Homewood Church of God in Pittsburgh, under the leadership of an extraordinary pastor, Elder E. D. Cobbs. There I found solace, strength, and hope. I gave my heart to the Lord, and He began to work with me in deep ways. In those dark and lonely nights, I would lay on my living room floor crying out and seeking the Lord for His purpose for my life.

There are defining moments in our lives, and it's so important to recognize the opportunity and take full advantage of the window given to us by God. Even in the midst of adversity and heartache, we can find solace in God's Word and the comfort of the Holy Spirit. As I reflect on years past, I can identify those defining moments. They were pivotal in my search to know God intimately. My insecurities and uncertainties were replaced with faith in the Word of God. I gained hope in His plan for my life and confidence in the will of God for the ministry He would birth in and through me. I was just a small-town girl with a great big God who entrusted me with a work. He would take to heights and depths I could never imagine.

I would learn to leave behind the negativity in my past and embark on a new and bright future with my son and my father. They would become my focus, and God's will for my life would become my purpose.

In spite of my mother's stern admonition, she could see my struggles and she was always there to encourage me and offer every ounce of support she could muster. She worked tirelessly and was always willing to assist me financially. She had not yet given her heart to the Lord, but she was wise enough to discern the call of God on my life. How was I to know God was using my struggles and His faithfulness to witness to Momma of His greatness and love that she would later embrace as her own?

My Brother's Addiction

When my brother returned from his tour of duty in Vietnam, he was addicted to drugs. He was unable to face life after being in the war. This was difficult for us to understand. Though our parents were separated, we were not raised in a chaotic environment. Rather, our home life was loving and nurturing. So our family was surprised when my brother came back home chemically dependent. We spent hours questioning the reason he was in this condition. We thought only dysfunctional people use drugs . . . right? We were not equipped to deal with this.

We did not know how to help him. Finally, he was arrested for a drug-related crime. Before he was taken to jail, he was unmercifully beaten in the street as they were putting him in the police car. We could not even recognize him when we visited the jail. His face and arms were so swollen, and his back was in a cast. They almost killed him! During the beating, they held a gun to his head. A woman looked out a nearby window and yelled, "If you pull that trigger, I will report that you shot this man when he was down." That may have been the only reason they did not kill him on the spot.

Seeking Help

My mother was devastated. She called one of the ministers of our church and asked if he would go to the jail to see my brother. He agreed. During the interview, he asked my brother, "If your mother gets you out of jail, will you break the law again?" Of course, my brother said, "No." He would have said anything to get out of jail!

I knew that Puddin would go back to using drugs! How could he not? He did not have the strength or the power to stop using—he was an addict! The minister really did not know what else to do or to say. That's when I asked God to please intervene. I begged Him to help my brother and my mother, and made myself available to be used not only to help my mother but also other mothers in pain.

Before I dealt with my brother's problem, I could not imagine how addicts and their family members suffered. It was foreign to me. We finally came up with the money to get my brother out of jail . . . and he went right back to using drugs! He could not help himself.

Before long, Puddin was in trouble again. His crimes were escalating. This time we heard the police had a warrant for his arrest and that, as soon as they found him, he was sure to be incarcerated. Puddin vowed he would kill himself before returning to prison, so he fled to another state. Sadly, years later his body was discovered in his California apartment. He died alone of an overdose—away from his family . . . away from everyone.

My mother received the call early one morning from a stranger who asked, "Is your name Margaret Bridges?" When she said yes, he bluntly continued, "Well, we have your son. We found him dead of an overdose."

My mother could not pull it together. She gave them my phone number because she could not comprehend what they were saying. And they told me the same thing in such a cold, harsh, matter-of-fact tone.

I believe God allowed me to experience this traumatic encounter so I would know the heartbreak people go through when they have a family member in trouble, especially because of chronic drug abuse. It is difficult for people who are in the midst of a crisis to know where to place the blame or find the answer. We have the tendency to blame ourselves and try to fix the problem with our own "fig leaves." That is where Peniel comes into the equation! We know who should claim the blame, and we stand ready to provide the only sure answer.

My Lifelong Calling

One day I went to visit my mother, who was then working as a school-crossing guard. She was standing on the corner waiting to escort the children safely through the busy streets on their way to school. As I approached her in her bright-yellow crossing guard uniform, she turned to me, and what I witnessed would change my destiny. She was weeping as she stood there. With tears streaming down her cheeks, she sobbed in a sadness that still haunts me.

Even though I already knew, I asked, "What's wrong, Momma?" I could see her deep sorrow and I understood why she was so distraught over the condition of my brother. He had fallen so low and she was helpless to know what to do to help him escape the addiction and its consequences.

At that moment, I knew my calling in life. I realized I must use every ounce of my being to find a solution. I must prevent another mother from this pain. There definitely was an answer; there had to be a solution to this problem. I did not know what it was, but God would soon reveal it in His time. The Lord had a plan—a path, a way of escape. If only it were not too late for my only brother, my friend, my confidant.

This was my brother, the one person who always came to my rescue. This was my mischievous brother who would watch me shell a bag of pistachios and, in a flash, grab all the spoils from my tired fingers. I embraced Momma and whispered, "It's going to be all right." Yet, my heart ached and my mind raced within me, searching for an answer to this question. Yes, indeed, the drug epidemic had become personal, and I would respond in kind.

As life would have it, even though the solution was available, Puddin did not take advantage of the opportunity. He eventually succumbed to the dark, relentless demons of his addiction, dying of an overdose on September 18, 1993. I am still weak in the knees, trying to accept that he would not allow himself to be saved. Even though God sent the answer in time, Puddin did not take advantage of it.

The Power of Influence

It is amazing what God will use to reinforce His message to His people. The movie *The Ten Commandments* had a powerful impact on my life. For weeks after seeing it, I was unable to sleep well. I could not overcome the wonder of knowing that a mere man could talk to God, and that God would respond. In fact, I was dealing with a God whom you could interact with on a personal level. That propelled my search for the *real* God. I knew what Charlton Heston portrayed in that movie was directly from the Scriptures, so it actually happened; but I did not have that type of relationship with God. Still, I desperately wanted it, and I began to seek God on another level.

Not long after that, I went to a revival to hear Sammy Ellis, a teenage evangelist, preach at the local Church of God. The fact that he was so young was a novelty, but he also had an experience with Almighty God.

After sensing that the Lord was dealing with me, he asked Reverend Arlene Bates and Reverend Lillian Bright to disciple me. Sister Bates was about two or three years old in the Lord at that time and Sister Bright was a seasoned Christian of many years. Both were on fire for God. To this day they continue to be used of God to preach, teach, and mentor young Christians. They laid the spiritual foundation in my life. I will forever be grateful to the Lord for using them. They were perfect teachers.

Patiently, they began to mentor me by modeling, teaching, and training me how to follow Christ. Sister Bates invited some of the young converts into her home for a weekly Bible study. She had five beautiful girls whom she raised to know and love the Lord. She would have Belinda, her youngest, on her lap as she expounded on the principles found in God's Word. Through their influence, many spiritual giants have found their place within the house of God and are serving Him until today.

Sister Bright would invite me to go house-to-house witnessing with her. She wanted me to see for myself the power of God at work. She was given a tremendous, even frightening gift of discernment, along with other obvious spiritual gifts. I would witness the indisputable move of God as she ministered to the people we visited. "What shall I do when we go inside?" I would ask as we approached the house that we were visiting.

"Watch . . . just watch!" she would sternly reply. So I watched! Confidentially, I was afraid to do anything else. I watched her skillfully get to the root of the matter of the troubled lives of those we visited. It appeared that it was always different than the obvious. After talking to the person for a while, she would clearly identify the problem, to their amazement. *How could she know?* would be the question on their faces. She would quickly give the glory to God. After clearly identifying the issues, she would invariably end up with the very same solution—Jesus, the Son of the living God, was the solution for all of humanity's ills.

The Jail Ministry

It was because of what was going on with my brother, I think, that I started volunteering at the local jail. Sister Arlene Bates and I teamed up and ministered at the Allegheny County Jail in Pittsburgh, Pennsylvania, for years. I was still relatively young in the faith, so it is more accurate for me to say that I accompanied Sister Bates to the jail, even though I asked her to go with me. This was quite an accomplishment, because Sister Bates felt called to minister to the Jewish community. Long after people left the church, she would weep at the altar for hours for those who did not know Jesus as Lord; that was her great burden. Somehow, I convinced her to go with me to the jails.

Actually, I knew she would go with me, because she could not pass up any opportunity to tell the story of God's love to anyone. So, she decided to go with me until her full-fledged ministry to the Jews materialized. *Whew!* Was I ever happy because she would be doing all the ministry. I would be there to pray while she preached. Who in this world could resist Sister Bates? She was, and is today, flat-out awesome.

We made an appointment to share our plan with Pastor Cobbs, who was one of the most dynamic speakers I have ever heard. Since we had the blessing of our pastor and the approval of the warden at the prison, we were set to go. And God used us in that prison beyond our expectation. Gangs were defeated, potential prison breaks were discovered, and lives were changed. But where were these new Christians to go to be discipled and placed once they were released? (It would be years later, and I did not know it then . . . but a Peniel was on the way.)

Today, Arlene Bates' daughter, Pamela, is carrying on the work her mom and I started many years ago. It has expanded to several prisons. How wonderful is that?

We would bring our converts to the local church, but the church was unable to address their needs. The common thread for most of those who were incarcerated was drug-and-alcohol addiction. That opened my eyes to see that in addition to the ministry of the church, something else was desperately needed as a support.

I got involved with a local Christian drug-treatment facility in our area, working there for several years. However, I always felt a loyalty to the Church of God. I believe if you belong to an organization, your loyalty is part of the deal. If you're in, then you need to be all the way in. I was part of the Church of God, and this church was part of me. It was the place I found the Lord. It was the place that fed me and helped me to change my life. I was committed.

Today, Spelly and I are humbly pastoring Lillian Bright and her daughter, Lydia. That's right! This giant in the ways of God is allowing us to pastor her. And I am still very nervous preaching when she is in the house!

The Divine Answer

Secular drug-and-alcohol treatment centers only have a 2 to 10 percent success rate. Talking about a "higher power" and using a positive-thinking approach have produced only temporary and short-lived success. What makes Peniel different?

Addiction can bring you to a place of despair and believing no one understands your pain. However, I know there is

One who loves us, who is in control, and knows what we go through. Our Lord understands every trial, and He has promised not to forsake us. We can bring all our sorrows to Him, regardless of how big or small they seem. There is hope *and* restoration for those who are addicted.

The formula for sustained sobriety has been a mystery to those receiving treatment, and even more so to those who are caught in the web of addiction on the streets. How can a young, single mother with little or no backing make a difference in our ongoing spiritual war against drug-and-alcohol addiction and the ravishing effects it has on families around the world?

The answer is a short one with long-reaching arms—it was personal for me and my family. I can recall the devastation of heroin addiction that gripped my brother and robbed him of his future and the potential that resided deep within his soul.

To our horror, many young men like my brother turned to heroin as a coping mechanism while serving in the jungles of Vietnam. When they returned to the States after a tour of duty, they brought their dependency with them, only to find a substandard product on the streets. This fueled an out-of-control addiction and intense desire for a drug that would satisfy their overwhelming craving. The war returned with them, except it was within.

God's Purpose

God certainly has His hand on my life, but I am not unique. I believe every man and woman was born with a divine purpose. Whatever the calling, if it comes from the mouth of God, it is distinctive and eternally rewarding.

Have you become conscious of the miracle of being a part of His divine plan? There is no need for you to wander without purpose or direction. There is a specific place for you in His house.

This letter was written by Marion Spellman (then "Coleman") just before the founding of Peniel.

WILLIAM B. ROBINSON
Commissioner

ERSKIND DERAMUS
Deputy Commissioner

PENNSYLVANIA BUREAU of CORRECTION
P. O. BOX 598
CAMP HILL, PENNSYLVANIA 17011
(717) 787-7480

February 13, 1980

Ms. Beckie Guyer
418 Oakland Street
Johnstown, PA 15902

Dearest Beckie:

I was just sitting here thinking of how blessed I am to have you as my very own daughter in the Lord. Sometimes we Mothers need to be a little more grateful for the children God has given us.

I desire that God will bless you with all the things that will make you strong in the Lord. And sometimes that means going thru the flood. But remember that the Lord hath said that it will not overflow you and if you go thru the fire you shall not be burned.

I was having devotions the other night and the Lord was so good to show me something that I thought might be a blessing to you. I have made it my prayer and perhaps you could get a blessing out of it also:

> Bind me, blessed Saviour, as a sacrifice-fasten me with Thy cords of constraining love lest I finish my course with shame. Let me not begin to make provision anywhere for the flesh-let my offering continue to be a burnt offering-a whole burnt offering, yea a continual burnt offering. Let me never come down from the cross to save myself. Fix me, fasten me, bind me with Thine own cords to Calvary, a continual burnt Offering.

It is my desire that the Lord will do something for us in this last day. I feel the need to work for Him greater than I have ever felt it before. I was thinking today what is it that He would have me to do for Him.

I feel that the Lord is calling me to something. I just don't really know what it is, but He (or let me say I was thinking today) what would I do if He asked me to quit my job.

Yes, I am actually, honestly thinking about quiting my job and going into full time work for Him. I feel the time running out and I know that only what I do for Jesus will last.

I would be bound to the cross, making no provision for the flesh and so I seek His will. Pray with me . Love,

M. Coleman

A Prodigal Finds Peniel

For years, while being actively involved in the music ministry of the church, I wasted my life. Promiscuous living and drug addiction nearly destroyed me. My wife gave up on me, as I failed to provide for her and my children. I was connected to the church but disconnected from God! I was in total denial, "having a form of godliness, but denying the power thereof" (2 Tim. 3:5).

Just as in the account of the Prodigal Son, I finally "came to myself" (see Luke 15:17). My life and my future were getting dimmer. I was tired of the negative lifestyle I was living. I didn't want to lose my family. Realizing I needed help, I called Mr. Henry Davis, who had earlier planted seeds during a conversation with me.

Those seeds fell on fertile ground. Mr. Davis directed me to Peniel on November 6, 1999. Since that day, my life has not been the same. I've come to know God not superficially but intimately! My wife and I have reconciled and have recommitted our lives to one another, putting God first.—*Corey (Maryland)*

CHAPTER 3

MY LOVE STORY

It was an extremely cold and windy day, with large snow banks lingering on the ground, when I received a follow-up phone call from Rev. Harold Palmer, a dear friend and a wonderful Church of God pastor. He had called a couple of days before about a young man from his congregation who had a severe drug addiction and was facing serious legal charges. The pastor said this troubled teenager had expressed a desire for Christian treatment.

"He is a young, spoiled, and very rebellious kid," Palmer said, "but deep down, I believe he is a fine young man. He comes from a good Christian family in our church, and we want to help him if at all possible."

In spite of the inclement weather, they were making their way to Peniel.

Because Peniel serves clients eighteen years and older, I had suggested that we refer sixteen-year-old Jonathan to another program in the area that specialized in treating clients fourteen years and over. Their facility was only an hour and a half away. I had scheduled the appointment and agreed to accompany them to the interview.

Upon arrival, we received a very cordial welcome from the director, Jeff, and his staff. We were then led to an office.

"Well, young man," Jeff kindly said as he sat down, "how can we help you?"

"I don't know!" Jonathan murmured, slouching in his seat and looking down at the floor.

"I understand you have a bit of a problem. I am told you have been using drugs and that you are seeking help. Is that right?" Jeff asked.

"*No*, that is not right!" Jonathan boldly responded.

Appearing confused, Jeff continued, "What am I missing? Did you just say *no*?"

"I said *no*!" Jonathan aggressively repeated. He was becoming more animated and speaking even louder!

"Then why are you here?" Jeff softly asked.

"They made me come! I want *nothing* to do with this!" He was now shouting.

Pastor Palmer was totally outdone! He looked as though someone had just punched him in the stomach. The pastor was finally able to get the words out of his mouth: "Are you serious? Why didn't you say this in the first place?"

"'Cause I didn't feel like it!" Jonathan belligerently responded. Now he was looking the pastor eye-to-eye in a threatening manner.

The room became silent until I chose not to contain my comments any longer. "Jonathan, look at me!" I said sternly. "Why are you so angry? You appear to be challenging your pastor. This is the man who has driven across the state to get you help and is willing to even pay for your treatment. What are you saying to us?"

"I don't want to be here!" Jonathan retorted. "I don't want treatment, I don't want your help, and I don't want God."

"And that's your choice," I said, intentionally interrupting, "but I am having trouble understanding why you waited until now to say this."

"Because I wanted to make a point to the pastor and to my family . . . to just leave me alone," he said. "*Just leave me alone.*"

"It's not going to happen, Jonathan! It's just not going to happen," I said softly. "And don't you dare smart off' at me. We will not insist that you receive this help, but we will never just let you go—you will be in our prayers.

"Jonathan, the road that you have chosen has led you to the steps of a burning house and your feet are already in the doorway. We are committed to doing all we can to prevent you from going in."

Jonathan kept his head down, but he did not speak again. He stood his ground with a stubborn silence. After a few other closing comments from the director, we gathered our things, thanked the staff, and sadly made our way to the car.

On the way back to Peniel, Pastor Palmer and I made small talk. We were deliberately trying to include Jonathan in the conversation and to assure him that we were not angry. Jonathan did not engage. Instead, he sat curled up in a corner of the backseat, defiantly sulking during the ride back to Peniel. Pastor and I were both saddened by the turn of events; still, we believed it was not over yet. We knew God would honor the prayers of Jonathan's parents and someday he would receive the help that he so desperately needed.

Harold Spellman was one of the staff members at that facility and was a part of the meeting with Jonathan. I was so focused on Jonathan's surprising attitude that I barely noticed him, and so I was shocked when Harold called me a few days later. He left this message on my answering machine: "This is Harold Spellman. We met the other day in the interview with Jonathan. I just called to say I am praying for you."

Praying for me? *What did he mean,* praying for me? *Who in the world was he, anyway?* I thought. *What a lame pickup line!*

A week later, he called again, and this time we spoke. At first, I wondered which one of the staff he was, but dared not reveal I did not recognize him! Still, he stuck to his flimsy story about praying for me, and I questioned where he was going with this. He went on to say he was disappointed with Jonathan's decision. We both agreed that this young man had made a poor choice.

Now we were running out of conversation, but I sensed he was not ready to hang up. As if searching for something else to talk about, he began telling me about a meeting that he and some of the residents from his center had attended at a local Assemblies of God church. He said the pastor had asked the congregation to pray for Peniel, a ministry that had recently opened. Harold said the pastor had given the congregation my name, and he wanted me to know that he too was praying for me. I went along with his story, but I sensed there was more to it than what he was saying. Finally, the call ended with me still unsure of its purpose.

As circumstances would have it, Harold's program and Peniel had already scheduled a joint recreational day at our facility. The plans were to have chapel together and then a meal, followed by residents participating in a softball game. Of course, Peniel won . . . although I am sure Spelly remembers this differently! It was at this gathering that I really saw Harold Spellman. He was tall, thin, and flat-out handsome! However, we said little to each other.

The following week, I was invited to speak at the New Life for Girls Treatment Center, where a good friend, Cookie Rodriguez, was the founding president and director. As we ate lunch, I mentioned that Harold Spellman had called me a few times.

"Marion, half of my ladies are praying that God will give him to them for a husband," Cookie said. "You're kidding!" I said. "Well, maybe his wife is here at New Life."

We both had a good laugh.

There was no reason for me to consider a romantic relationship, let alone the possibility of marriage. In my heart, this matter had been settled. I had been through a painful divorce, and my ex-husband had long since left me and our son. He was living with another woman even before the marriage was officially over. I had resolved to allow the Lord to completely heal me and was prepared to commit the rest of my life to His work. I was devoted to raising my son and caring for my sick father. I was content with my life.

As for Harold, since he would soon be moving to Minneapolis, Minnesota, to attend Bible college, speaking to him on the phone posed no real threat. Harold was very serious about the things of God. He was kind and an absolute gentleman at all times. He had a deep respect for women and he never crossed boundaries. Most of our conversations centered on the Scriptures and his being spiritually prepared to leave for college. Nevertheless, as a precaution, at first we limited our interaction to phone calls. Eventually, we started seeing each other in public places like shopping malls and restaurants.

We also started attending evening church services together. At one of those meetings in a non-denominational church in York, Pennsylvania, Pastor Thomas Loudon abruptly interrupted his message by pointing his finger toward Harold.

"Come forth, young man," he said. "I strongly feel led to confirm that God has a special work for you. You will reach many people, and many lives will be eternally changed because of your ministry. You will return to the area from which you have been delivered, and God will bless. You will do a great work."

The pastor then anointed Harold and prayed for him. He did not know Harold or me, and it was surprising he even noticed our presence. This experience was very encouraging, yet somewhat frightening.

As his phone calls became more frequent, I could not deny that I was experiencing a growing concern about what was happening within my heart as it related to Mr. Harold Spellman. Although I was impressed with his love and commitment to God and his gratitude for what the Lord had done in his life, still I wondered if I was beginning to move in a sinful direction.

Gradually, our conversations turned to discussions of the scriptures regarding divorce and remarriage. *Why are we even talking about this?* I asked myself. *What is the real purpose of this relationship? Certainly this not God's will for me.* Acting like a good Christian, I halfheartedly prayed, "God, please help me! I don't want to sin against You."

God is so faithful, especially in our folly. God indeed answers prayer even when they are less than totally sincere. It was as if someone shook me and said, "Come on, Marion! Come on out of your state of denial! It's time for you to get brutally honest."

The truth was, I was falling in love with Harold Spellman!

Everything was at stake! I was already struggling as a black woman in a white man's world. I had often felt the sting of being overlooked and in some cases merely tolerated in circles where I was clearly qualified to have a voice. I would be out of my mind to open a controversial discussion about my personal life. This would take the focus off the work God had ordained for me to do. Was this the devil trying to derail me when my immediate goal was to build community goodwill?

There was also another possibility—perhaps Satan was trying to use me to hinder God's purpose for Harold's life—that thought frightened me to my core. I felt a sense of desperation to have this matter resolved!

God had already brought me through the indescribable pain of a bad marriage. I had no intention of leaving the God to whom I was so indebted just for a romance with a man with a handsome face. My relationship with God was worth far more to me than the risk of compromising His call on my life.

Within a few days, without my speaking to Harold about my feelings or spiritual concerns, he said to me, "We need counsel! God has brought me too far for me to blow it now. God has brought me out of Egypt, and I'm not going back there for anyone or anything!"

Now we're talking! I thought. I wish I could express the peace I felt when Harold spoke those words to me. For the first time in my life, I felt completely safe and secure with a mere man. I was talking to a man who was able to make hard decisions about what he believed—a man committed to God before he would give himself to any woman.

"Here is what we will do," Harold said. "We will choose seven spiritual and influential people in our lives, and if any one of them objects to our relationship, we will discontinue it on the spot! It will only take one person to object."

Together we chose them: (1) Harold's mother, Sarah Spellman (Harold's father was deceased); (2) Mike Fletchinger, Harold's director and spiritual adviser; (3) Reverend Carl Scott, Harold's pastor and spiritual father; (4 & 5) my mother and my father; (6) Pastor E. D. Cobbs, my spiritual father; and (7) Reverend Jerry Tow, my present pastor (who married us).

I had some concerns about how our spiritual fathers would respond. Harold's pastor barely knew me. Pastor Scott meant so much to Harold that I don't believe Harold would have gone against his opinion had he disapproved. However, after reviewing all of the information regarding the breakup of my marriage and my ultimate divorce, Pastor Scott gave us his blessings. What a relief!

Although I had cried on Elder Cobbs' shoulders for years, I did not think he would approve of my relationship with Harold. We saved our session with him for last. In the meantime, we met with everyone else on our list, and they all said they would support this relationship. They wished us happiness and promised to pray for us.

After the pleasantries were over in our meeting with Elder Cobbs, Harold said to him, "Marion and I would like to take our relationship to another level. We have come to ask for your blessing."

"When you say 'another level,'" Elder Cobbs asked gently, "what does that mean?"

"We have been discussing the Bible's position regarding remarriage, and we think that Marion is eligible—but we may not be objective, so we need to hear from you," Harold concluded.

There was a loud silence. The atmosphere was saturated with anticipation and anxiety. Finally, after what felt like an eternity, looking Harold directly in his eyes, Elder Cobbs slowly, softly, and deliberately spoke: "I believe God is in this thing."

I couldn't believe it . . . I still can't believe it! But what he said was true, and after all these many years, we are still declaring God is in this thing!

We accepted the responses from those who had proven to care for our souls as the Lord's blessing for us to marry and to know God would be with us. Yes! God would bless our joint effort to serve and honor Him for the rest of our lives. I think Spelly said it best in his book, *Images, Idols and Other High Places*:

> We recognized that our getting married meant rethinking some things and reorganizing some priorities. For example, we both realized that I could not go off to Bible college in Minnesota. It was equally clear that we could not work in two different ministries and accomplish what we felt God was saying to us. We knew that God was creating a ministerial team to maximize our potential.
>
> On June 5, 1981, at twelve noon on a beautiful summer day, with the assurance that God was directing us, Marion and I were joined together in holy matrimony. After a brief honeymoon, we returned to Peniel to begin our journey. Our immediate goal was to make Peniel Ministries a successful drug/alcohol program in both the Christian and in the non-Christian community (Treasure House, Shippensburg, Pa.).

Now that the honeymoon is over and it's more than three decades later, we can still boldly proclaim that God continues to fulfill every promise and supply every need. The Lord is such a wonderful Savior. Just this morning, Spelly and I were gratefully reminiscing about the faithfulness of God in our lives. It is overwhelming when we stop to think of the battles we have fought and won through Him. Indeed, God has brought us through family fatalities, personal life-threatening illnesses, financial reversals, painful betrayals, and attacks against our integrity and our leadership. And, yes, the big one—Satan has been relentless in trying to rob us of our cherished peace, joy, and confidence. But, praise God, we are still standing, still holding on to Him, and we are still together!

God has used even the smallest details to confirm His plan for our lives. Who would have thought that after moving throughout most of the state in search of a home, the very place we honeymooned (Johnstown) would be the future headquarters for this ministry!

Surely, I want to shout it from the highest mountain that we can totally trust God's will for our lives. No good thing will He withhold from us. If God has closed a door in your life, don't force the issue. Wait on the perfect will of God! He always has something in mind for our lives.

Highlighting my love story with you has been a joy, but I don't want to close this chapter without sharing a few moments with Spelly and me as we prepare to go on a trip. You will get to know us a little bit better. . . .

Harold and Marion Spellman

"Hon, do you see my red coat in the car? It's not in the closet," I call out to Spelly from the bedroom upstairs.

"No, Babe, your coat is not in the car. Don't you have another one you can take?"

"Oh, now I remember!" I answer. "I left it in my office. Will you please run over to the center and get it for me? I'll be ready by the time you get back."

A few minutes pass, and then I hear Spelly open the front door. "OK, Babe. I've got the coat."

"Thanks, Hon; just hang it up in the closet in the playroom and I'll be right down."

"Hang it up? Hang it up?" he asks again, as if he did not hear himself the first time. "I thought you wanted to take it with you!"

"I did at first, but while you were gone, I realized my long black coat will be more appropriate."

You have never heard a more deafening silence in your life. Then the all-too-familiar words ring out from the bottom of the stairs: "Marion, I thought you said you were ready."

"I am . . . I am," I impatiently reply. "I'm coming! Spelly, just give me a minute. . . . Oh, Hon, I need you to put this cream in my brown cosmetic bag," I continue. "It will fit with no problem at all."

"Marion," my frustrated husband responds, "the suitcases are already in the car. Didn't I ask you to p-l-e-a-s-e pack everything that you would need in advance—and didn't you specifically tell me last night that everything was packed?"

With a deep sigh, or maybe an exasperated groan, and without wanting or expecting an answer, he continues his chastising: "How many times do I have to ask you to *please, please* pack everything you need the night before?"

Now I am intentionally ignoring his aggravating questions, and I purposely refocus his attention with a demanding question of my own: "Harold Spellman, what in the world is this attitude about? Are you going to put this stuff in my bag or not?"

My voice tone purposely communicates I am the one who is upset here, and furthermore, I am also very offended.

Bulls-eye! He picks up the vibe! "OK, Marion, just give it to me! I hope this jar is gonna fit in that small bag, because we are absolutely not taking one more piece of luggage."

Then, he continues mumbling as he takes the must-have cleansing cream, the forgotten slippers, and the just-in-case extra pair of jeans that I conveniently slipped in. Giving one final check to assure the lid is screwed on tightly, he continues to make inaudible mumbling noises—sounds that he alone can utter!

As he walks toward the car, I see the trunk had been left wide open, because he knew I would surely forget something. Chuckling to myself, I think, *Why does he put himself through all this aggravation every single trip?*

Trying to make the situation a little better, I halfheartedly ask, "Can I help you with the bags, Hon?" Bad timing! Wrong question! He looks at me as if I am speaking in another language and defiantly refuses to answer.

With a fasten-your-seatbelt reminder, we are finally on our way. It is completely quiet in the car and his breathing is slowly coming back to normal. After what seems to be forever, he says, "Are you hungry, or do you just want to wait until we get to Breezewood?" Without saying another word, he smiles and visibly affirms all is well between us.

The trip promises to be long and exhausting, but we both feel a sense of anticipation and excitement. We are eager to take full advantage of this opportunity to be alone together. It is our time to just talk.

We talk about everything, and we talk about nothing. We discuss the latest family crisis and how we should respond. Next, we shift to the problems of Peniel, the victories and the heartaches happening within our church. We discuss politics a little bit and then agree to put that subject on the back burner for now. We share precious moments of absolute silence, and we chatter like teenagers about silly stuff.

No matter what we discuss, our conversations invariably lead us to biblical principles. God's recorded mind-set on every matter influences us to either make an attitude adjustment or reinforce God's position on the subject.

His Word never, ever, fails! Even as we are speaking about something absolutely unrelated, the Holy Spirit is certain to prick my heart with a sense of shame and genuine repentance. I speak softly as I slowly reach for his hand. "I'm sorry that I upset you this morning, Hon. I'm really going to do better."

"No, Babe," he gently interrupts, "I am the one who is sorry. I'm sorry I wasn't more patient with you. My behavior was unacceptable and unnecessary."

We smile at each other and he tenderly squeezes my hand. Still, deep inside, I suspect that we both know this scene is sure to play out again. However, we always have the hope that we will get it right the next time.

Does this incident sound familiar? You have a bird's-eye view of a moment in the life of the Spellmans. We sometimes face family conflicts that are far more serious, but the solution is always the same: earnestly repent, courageously accept responsibility, genuinely forgive, and then make needed adjustments.

The question is, Can a healthy, loving relationship exist or even grow where disagreement, disappointment, or confusion are possible and even inevitable? Does it matter if spurts of disharmony or even manipulation occur between family, friends, or spouses? Frustration, friction, and conflict are all common in relationships, but biblical principles always remain and must ultimately prevail.

Let's settle some basic particulars about love. There is *true love*, and then there is something that masquerades as love. This spirit is manifested by sensual thrills, self-gratification, and earthly passions. Its formal name is *lust*. It declares itself to be legitimate, when it is really a barefaced, unadulterated, bogus abuser. Lust's greatest tools are *deception* and *camouflage*. In far too many relationships, lust is chosen over true love because it does not demand the same effort, promise the same pain, nor require the same commitment.

Self-serving fraud claims will ultimately demand all, give nothing, and always leave its victims wanting. They are as far from genuine love as the east is from the west . . . we dare not settle for lust on any level.

Unfortunately, "I love you" is often sadly reduced to a misused cliché. Unless and until we accurately identify, distinctly characterize, and conspicuously experience the awesome love of God, we will never know what we are looking for or if we have even found it.

Stand secure on the truth that "God is love" (1 John 4:8). In 1 Corinthians 13, we see what love looks like:

> Love suffers long and is kind; love does not envy; love does not parade itself, is not puffed up; does not behave rudely, does not seek its own, is not [easily] provoked, thinks no evil; does not rejoice in iniquity, but rejoices in the truth; bears all things, believes all things, hopes all things, endures all things. Love never fails. But whether there are prophecies, they will fail; whether there are tongues, they will cease; whether there is knowledge, it will vanish away. . . . And now abide faith, hope, love, these three; but the greatest of these is love (vv. 4-8, 13 NKJV).

I could say more on this subject of *love*, but Spelly and I are on our way to a state conference . . . and I have to go upstairs and pack.

Ushered Into a Good Life

In August 1990, a friend asked me if I wanted to try crack cocaine. There was an older man present who said, "If you take a hit of this poison, you will be hooked!" That man was so right!

In 2003, after reaching my lowest point, I finally asked God if He would give me another chance, I would put Him first in my life. I knew I needed help, and I could not do it on my own. At Peniel, I learned to have daily devotions—reading my Bible and praying to God. Also, I learned to stay focused, stay in prescribed boundaries, be accountable, and make the right choices.

Today, God is the head of my life, I have my family back, and I have been sober for eleven years with no desire to return to a life of addiction. I am a member of the Pentecostal Church of God in Christ in Pittsburgh. Also, I am a member of the Usher Board, and I enjoy "ushering" others into the house of the Lord.—*Milton (Pennsylvania)*

CHAPTER 4

NOTHING LESS THAN THE BEST

On a cold winter day in February 1981, Peniel opened its doors for two male residents. It would be more than six years before Peniel would be large enough to accept females. The facility was located in the small community of Dillsburg, Pennsylvania.

The cherry-wood cabins we occupied had been used exclusively as a summer dinner theater, so they had not been insulated against the harsh winds and snow that blew through the cracks between the logs. To keep warm, we used wood-burning stoves and kerosene heaters. We took the heavy green drapes off the windows to use as blankets for the clients' cots, which had been donated. We did whatever we could afford to transform the place into a drug-and-alcohol treatment facility.

We promptly invited the community to join this effort by donating financial and material gifts. Some of the discarded items left by the previous owners were carefully examined, and when appropriate, cleaned up and reused. We never took the position of being disadvantaged; we were grateful God had called us to minister. Unknowingly, we were doing what

Dillsburg Property

Secretary's First Office

others said was impossible. What a sense of accomplishment to make things work that had been labeled *useless*.

Becki Guyer, one of our founding staff members, was my "right hand." She is extremely artistic, and she excelled at creating something out of nothing.

Let me describe our first clients. We went to the inner city and pulled aside three older guys who looked like they could use help from anyone. We asked them if they wanted to come to Peniel instead of living on the streets, and they said yes. We piled them in the car and were on our way with our first clients . . . but when we got to the center and told them they had to bathe and turn in their cigarettes, that was the end of that! They were having nothing to do with a bath, and they certainly were not giving up their cigarettes.

"Take us back; we will stay at the mission," they said.

Disappointed, we took them back. *What did we do wrong?* we wondered. *Were we asking too much? Should we have been more gradual about telling them to bathe and not to smoke in this Christian program designed to help them clean up their lives?* No! The bathing rule remained, and this would continue to be a no-smoking facility. There would be no compromise.

We maintained the integrity of the vision, and God honored us for our stance. The clients came in and the number of residents began to grow. God was blessing lives, restoring families, reuniting marriages, and salvaging souls. The vision, which had previously been only a dream on paper, was now becoming a reality.

The $500 rental fee we were paying for the property was astronomical, since we had begun operation with an account balance of 35 cents. As a newly organized ministry, we were trying feverishly to establish a reputation of honor and integrity. We were asking people to believe in our work enough to invest in us. How we thank God today for those individuals who blindly stepped out in faith to support our work on a monthly basis. We learned how to "borrow from Peter to pay Paul," and we were meeting our expenses . . . but barely!

A Church of God Ministry

Clearly the ministry was to be under the leadership of a spiritually sound, established, and honorable organization. Peniel had to be rooted in something much greater than the Spellmans. The goal was for the work of the Lord to continue beyond any one individual. Believing in the Church of God and its doctrine, I was sure God had called this ministry specifically for this particular church to nurture and grow.

I shared this mandate with my pastor and our state overseer, and I would tell people, "This is a Church of God ministry." But when they called our church headquarters in Cleveland, Tennessee, to inquire about Peniel, they would hear, "We don't even know about this ministry, and we do not know Marion Spellman."

This didn't faze me. I still continued to declare that Peniel indeed was a Church of God ministry. Since then, I have come to understand the denomination's position in this matter was not personal. They honestly did not know me or the work I was doing. As responsible leaders, they would not sanction anyone or anything they didn't know. They were a worldwide ministry, and I am so grateful for the position our leadership took. I needed that experience because it challenged my call. Was I really called, or was I called only if I was recognized by an organization?

God tapped into that get-the-job-done spirit He placed in me and demanded that I refuse to lose my vision. He forced me to depend on Him and not on organizations. With all of that, it was clear to me that the ministry was to remain under the leadership, doctrine, and requirements of the Church of God. They just didn't know it yet, but they would. God promised me they would.

Meeting the Executive Council

For the graduation service one year, we invited Bishop Raymond Crowley, who was the general overseer, to be our keynote speaker. I was shocked when he accepted the invitation. Upon arrival, God touched his heart when he saw the work we were doing. He then invited me to go to Cleveland to introduce the Church of God Executive Council to the ministry of Peniel.

The invitation was an honor, but being unfamiliar with the politics of the church, I did not realize this was a big deal. Nor did I realize I would have a private audience with the governing body of the denomination. I went to Cleveland without any fear or nervousness about the visit. I looked the committee members in the eyes and said, "You guys have a 'baby' up in Pennsylvania you are not taking care of. You aren't even claiming it, but it's still your baby. It looks like you, walks like you, talks like you, and is carrying your name. Whether you claim this baby or not, it belongs to you."

Certainly, I would not have been so bold had I understood who I was addressing. The Council was composed of men like Dr. Ray Hughes, Dr. John Nichols, Dr. Raymond Crowley, and the list goes on; but I didn't know the power in that room. As I talked to them about Peniel, the room was silent. When I finished, Dr. Crowley asked, "What would you have us to do?"

In reality, I only wanted their blessing. Anything more was in the hands of God. Maybe the Lord blinded me so I would allow them to see the real Marion Spellman and the burden He had deposited in my heart. We officially became a Church of God ministry that day.

At Last There's Hope

If I didn't believe God's Word has the power to completely reverse addictive behavior, I would pack up my office and walk away. However, I know many of the broken people who walk through the doors of Peniel have godly parents, grandparents, and loved ones who have prayed, fasted, and believed God for their salvation. For some, it is their last-chance of hope for freedom from their addiction. They have tried everything they know and have failed miserably.

The need to touch hurting men and women has gained momentum over recent years. Peniel provides a refuge where they can work through the self-esteem issues and chronic addictions that plague them. It is a place where credentialed staff utilize the infallible Word of God and proven treatment tools to patiently walk them through the devastating maze of their world.

Every time I walk through the doors of Peniel, I am reminded of our purpose statement—"At Last There's Hope." This hope is rooted in Jesus Christ and the appropriate and efficient sobriety tools.

Velvet and Steel

As the founder of Peniel, I have been challenged regarding my role. I don't believe there is a conflict with me being a combination of "velvet" and "steel." I have rejected the label of being "aggressive" simply because my job requires me to present strong opinions and express godly insight. I would never sacrifice my femininity for position or power.

Recently, I attended a seminar designed exclusively for women executives. Most of the two hundred participants were heads of large corporations or managers of big business firms. Although these women had reached the apex of their professions, classroom feedback revealed that many of them were in some type of bondage, whether it was because of unreasonable demands, unfair treatment, or unkind labeling.

The not-so-subtle message of today's society disregards God's design for women. Hollywood depicts women as aggressive superwomen who practice ungodly and inappropriate behavior, often concealing their damaged and fragile hearts. However, I believe God ordains, blesses, and leads Christian women into a variety of ministry arenas.

Often the women who come to Peniel are struggling to find their identity. They may be unable to make a basic decision or they may have to be in total control. Our goal at Peniel is to bring these hurting women to the point where they can admit, "Yes, I'm hurting. I'm alone, I feel rejected, and I need help." Only then can they move on and say, "I'm forgiven, and I can make it. I have purpose and peace as long as I submit to the will of God for my life."

Licensure Required

When Becki told me that Joe Powell from the Pennsylvania Department of Drug and Alcohol Programs was on the phone asking for the person who was in charge, I cheerfully answered, "Good morning, Mr. Powell. This is Marion Spellman. How can I help you?"

"Good morning, Mrs. Spellman. I represent the Department of Drug and Alcohol Programs. It has been brought to our attention that you are running a drug program. Is that true?"

"Yes, indeed," I said, thinking this was another opportunity to share this wonderful vision with someone new. He was looking for the facts, and I was the one to give them to him. I went into my persuasion mode and told him how Peniel was born in my heart as a result of my brother's battle with drugs. I told him how we started with no up-front money, but had enlisted the help of several caring people, and *yes* . . . we were operating as a bona fide drug-and-alcohol program.

Mr. Powell quietly listened. He did not interrupt, except to say an occasional *um-hum*, or *I see*, or *yes*. Toward the end of my pitch, I began to feel a little uneasy. *Maybe I have misjudged the purpose of this call,* I thought. Finally, I asked, "Does this familiarize you with our program?"

"Yes," he said kindly. "Thank you. It sounds like you have a commendable passion for those who are addicted. I have to tell you, though, you are not permitted to operate a drug program without being licensed."

"Licensed? How do I obtain a license?"

"I will send you the regulations. I will put them in the mail today."

"OK, that will be great," I said. "And thank you!"

"You are more than welcome," he said as we ended the conversation.

Within a couple of days, a large package arrived. As I opened it and breezed through the regulations, I began to hyperventilate. It may as well have been written in Hebrew! I could not make heads or tails of the sections and subsections. All of the *heretofores* and the *not limited to's* and the *moreovers* were unbelievable. I did not have a clue what they were saying, let alone what they required.

I promptly picked up the phone and called the number on the cover sheet. "May I speak with Mr. Joe Powell, please?" I asked.

"One moment, I will see if he is in," someone said politely.

"This is Mr. Powell," he said.

"Mr. Powell," I said with confidence. "This is Marion Spellman. I spoke with you earlier."

"Yes, Marion, did you get the packet?"

Well, I thought, *this is good. He has called me Marion. He is probably approachable, but I would not cross the line with him.* "Mr. Powell, I need help interpreting your stipulations."

He chuckled and said, "I'm sure it is confusing, but we have field techs who are assigned to assist the directors. I will help you understand and address the regulations." And he did.

Mr. Powell was tough. He would not settle for anything but perfection. He would return a document as many times as it took to get it right. He refused to do it for me, but he was there to guide me.

This was one of the most difficult experiences of my ministry, but God would use it to ground this ministry in excellence. I finally addressed all of the regulations enough to get a provisional license. Mr. Powell and the people in the department were still not satisfied. For several inspections, we could not receive a higher score than for provisional license, which meant Peniel was given only six months to bring up the many areas that were in noncompliance.

When we improved one area, they found another that was deficient. Every inspection was a different agent, and each one found another violation. This was all leading up to the "biggie"—the actual property. We were cited to bring the entire facility up to meet the standard, or we would have to move.

All this time, I knew Mr. Powell did not swear, was very cordial and polite, and had a nonaggressive but firm personality. I knew he was professional, always insisting on excellence, but I did not know he was a devout Christian and a leader in his church. Years passed before I discovered he was a man of great faith.

"Woman of the Year" Award

Eventually, I came to realize Joe Powell had been handpicked and sent by God to demonstrate things I would need to know in the future. His uncompromising demand for excellence was God's plan and path for Peniel. Joe Powell's everlasting requests to "please resubmit that document with the corrections we discussed" was God's method of establishing a nothing-less-than-the-best approach for Peniel . . . no matter how many resubmissions it took.

Sometime after Mr. Powell was promoted and no longer worked directly with programs on the field, his church honored me with its "Woman of the Year" award. It meant more to me than the audience would ever know. For me, it was Joe Powell's affirmation of my efforts, although he would never acknowledge that. His attitude was, "I am here to help anyone who needs me." He would never do anything for me to think I was special, so I decided to believe I was just very blessed. That morning I was the guest speaker at his church, and I was very comfortable preaching God's Word. But I don't know what I said when it was time to accept the award—all I remember is I could not hold back the tears.

I am happy to report that for several years of annual inspections, conducted by the Department of Health and Offices of Drug and Alcohol Programs, our center has received perfect scores. Thank you, Joe Powell. Thank you for never accepting less than our best.

My Message

Discernment plays an important role in acquiring a lasting freedom. Just as the disciples were initially unable to discern the freedom Jesus offered—a freedom that transcended Roman tyranny—so it is with many people today. Jesus taught that scriptural guidelines for behavior are not optional. Whether a person is a believer or an unbeliever, those who resist obeying the Word of God will experience unrest. Outwardly, they may appear satisfied, but inwardly they are vagabonds in quest of freedom. My message to them is they are being held captive by the Enemy who has already been defeated at Calvary.

At one time, the staff at Peniel worked closely with a young man in a federal penitentiary who was serving four consecutive life sentences. Because of his bitter attitude, he was sentenced to solitary confinement for seven years. During that time, he was not permitted to speak to anyone other than prison officials. He suffered several mental breakdowns because of the isolation.

When he was placed back with the general prison population, he began planning his escape. He believed if he could be free from prison, he would be free indeed. The Holy Spirit used my husband, Spelly, to help this young man see his imprisonment was not the foundational source of his problem. Through a booklet I had written titled *Just in Time*, he learned he needed to be free within. Eventually, he came to experience the saving power of the Lord Jesus Christ.

My greatest desire is to show people the way to overcome external pressures and to know happiness is not by acquiring a different mate, a different house, more money, or a different church; their critical need is to find contentment in Christ through a deep commitment to Him.

To our shame, many of God's children are in bondage. Some have been shackled so long that freedom becomes a threat. They rationalize it is better to suffer under the taskmasters of Egypt than to conquer the giants and possess the land of liberty. They even scoff at those who exercise their faith. Like a bird without a song, they are unable to function effectively . . . and will ultimately perish for lack of purpose.

Finding freedom is no great mystery. The Holy Spirit performs the work, releasing those who are bound in accordance with the stipulations set forth by Jesus Christ. When Jesus drank the bitter cup at His crucifixion, He conquered every reason for a person to be enslaved. When He descended to the uttermost parts of the earth as our invincible champion over death, hell, and the grave, He set at liberty those who were held captive. Today He holds the keys that will unlock any prison door.

Casting all shame and guilt at the feet of Jesus, captives will hear the glorious words of authority that only Christ can proclaim: "Loose them and let them go free!" I am dedicated to echoing that statement of deliverance to men and women everywhere—today and every day!

Now a Prison Chaplain

Prior to Peniel I was a lost, undone junkie. After ten years of hell on earth, dragging my wife and son down with me, I overdosed and almost died. I was pushing away the ones that I love most, but God got my attention! After hitting rock-bottom, I cried out for help! The door was opened for me to go to a God-sent ministry called Peniel.

While in treatment, through godly counsel and mentorship, my eyes were opened to how much Christ loved me. Even during the time I was in my addiction, God loved me and cared for me.

Now I am a man of God, a husband to my beautiful wife, and a father to my child. I am a chaplain who works in prison ministry with recovering addicts. God has opened door after door. I thank God every day for Peniel, where I saw God's love with my own eyes. I graduated in 2012. God's love through Peniel changed my life forever!—*Matt*

CHAPTER 5

DISCOVERING THE MIND OF GOD

The coming days would present tremendous testing for Spelly and me, which we later realized were designed to boost our confidence in God and take us to a new and glorious level. Our heavenly Father had laid a firm foundation within our spirits, without which we would have never been equipped to withstand the battle before us. We were learning how to utilize spiritual tools that had proven repeatedly to work for the people of God.

Our daily devotions were precious. This time spent with Spelly was nonnegotiable. We would marvel each time we read about God miraculously opening the Red Sea and leading His people out on totally dry land . . . right in the face of their enemies. We never tired of reading about the blind receiving their sight, or the lame being able to walk.

We inhaled God's Word and stood boldly on His promises. These biblical accounts we read every day were establishing His infallible and unadulterated truth within our heart. Indeed, there is no challenge on earth that is beyond the power of God. During those special devotional moments, God would wrap us tightly in His presence. The problems had not changed, but God was changing *us*, which was His plan from the beginning.

Spelly and I were en route from a promotional meeting in York, Pennsylvania, about an hour from the center, when out of the blue, I was terrified. I said, "Spelly, quick—find a telephone booth! I need to call the center; something is desperately wrong at Peniel." It is still hard for me to accurately explain the sensation I was experiencing, but a strong spirit of fear overwhelmed me. However, I did know this: "God has not given us a spirit of fear, but of power and of love and of a sound mind" (2 Tim. 1:7 NKJV).

While Spelly pulled up to the nearest telephone booth, and with the coins in hand, I jumped out of the car and dialed the center. After her warm and professional greeting, and as soon as my secretary realized the call was from me, her tone of voice changed. She blurted out, "We are in big trouble! The electric guy was here to turn off the power! We pooled together $30, which was all of the money we had, and gave it to him. He said he would delay shutting off our power, but only until 5 o'clock."

I simply said to Becki, "We are on our way! We should be there in about twenty minutes."

I was shaking on the inside when we arrived. I spoke to no one and went straight to my office to add up the receipts for the money that had come in that week. My quick estimate was it should be close to $400 or $500. I gathered all of the deposit-slip carbons and began entering the figures into the adding machine. The total was much more than I thought; yet it was still not enough. *I had better add them one more time, just to be sure*, I thought.

Then I called in Becki and nervously added the figures again, and to our amazement, the total was even more! This time I asked her to call out the figures to me. I could not believe it—the total was even greater! Then I called out the numbers to her . . . and the figure had increased again! Yes, we were in the midst of a miracle!

S-l-o-w-l-y and nervously, I added the deposit slips a final time. The total had increased so much that we had more money on paper than we needed. I didn't question if the figures were accurate or not; I chose to believe Peniel was experiencing a divine intervention. So I quickly wrote the check for the appropriate amount.

Deposit Continues to Increase

Spelly took the payment to the utility office. As he pulled up, he saw the electric company had just closed and the woman was walking to her car. Spelly asked her if she would be willing to go back inside to receive our check. She said, "Ordinarily I would not reopen, but I will do it for you." The figure we had totaled from the escalating deposit slips was confirmed by our bank. God is awesome!

We gathered in the chapel to offer thanksgiving to the one true and living God. A rejuvenating spirit of revival broke out! God had moved on our behalf, and everyone at Peniel knew it! We praised Him for His great faithfulness toward us. We had just defeated a formidable foe, and we were determined to take the time to openly glorify God and thereby set an example to those in our care. We taught our students to apply scriptural responses to blessings received from God.

In the meantime, wonderful friends who believed in the vision of Peniel came alongside us with their prayerful and financial support, including Dick Burns, who pastored the Oakland United Methodist Church in Johnstown. From the beginning, he supported Peniel faithfully, always encouraging his people to give. His unforgettable words were, "Marion

Spellman, I cannot do what you do, but we will pass the ammunition." As I write this book, it has been more than thirty years, and the Oakland United Methodist Church continues to support Peniel.

Another example is Dave and Cyndy Watters. Even though we lost Dave a few years ago, Cyndy has continued to honor their commitment to support Susan, who is now my secretary. Neither Dave nor Cyndy ever expected applause; her monthly gift is always on time, and she is faithful to remember Peniel when she prays.

Then there is Debby Khuri—an extraordinarily beautiful woman of God who could write a couple of chapters about the sufferings of Job. Debby has had more back-to-back deaths in her immediate family than one would ever imagine a person could endure. Yet, when you meet this intelligent, elegant, soft-spoken former schoolteacher, you will not detect a hint of bitterness. What a giant in the Lord she is! We are thrilled she became a member of the Peniel Praise Community Church.

Another dear friend of Peniel is Pat Brantley. From the time we met, the Brantleys have always been available. Bishop Mike and Pat are the pastors of an exciting and growing church in Kentucky. Pat is one of the most positive people I have ever known. She and her husband have a burning passion for the Peniel clients. Often we would learn that the Brantleys were giving out of their personal need; in fact, you will never see an individual as happy as Pat is to trust God in her giving. Pat's testimony is that their new home is a direct response for the seeds she has planted in this ministry.

These are just a few of the people God sent to keep us encouraged and to maintain our focus. However, tests kept coming.

We once faced a rent increase of a million dollars. Well, not quite a million, but it felt like it. Actually, it was $500. The landlord insisted that we pay the additional increase each month or we would have to move. At the same time, a printing company called to demand full and immediate payment of $1,500 for newsletters that had recently been completed.

They were threatening litigation that would demand our bank to freeze our account.

Feeling numb, I went into my office and slowly closed the door. I reached for our financial folder to review our recent deposits, and I began to enter them on the adding machine. This was easy to do because they were all in order and meticulously listed. *Well*, I thought, *if neatness would do it, we've got it made.* We needed another miracle! God had done it before—He could do it again.

Why was the number *2,000* always plaguing me? When would the Lord raise up enough finances for us to do the work He had called us to do? We had developed a newsletter because we wanted to get the word out about Peniel. We used a professional printer because God had taught us to do things well. Looking up, I said, "Help us pay these people . . . *please*!"

There! All the figures were in. My fingers trembled as I reached out to touch the "total" key. One punch of the button and I would have the bottom line. Were we about to see the figures multiply again? Somehow I found the courage to push that button. There it was—the devastating news was before me. It was even worse than I had thought.

How could we have stayed afloat this long? And with the immediate financial demands, I did not know what to think. One thing was sure: Unless God saw something I couldn't see, I was experiencing the death of Peniel—it was just a matter of time.

What if the ministry closed? What would our enemies say about the power of God? What would this do to the staff's faith? Would Satan arise victoriously and more powerful? I probably should start looking for appropriate placements for our clients. This was just too much! It was too overwhelming for me to handle.

As I sat back and settled myself, it was as if the Lord had been sitting in the chair across the room observing me. He was silently hearing and, yes, just watching me. It was almost as if He said, "Now, may I speak?"

"Yes, Lord, speak," I replied. "Your servant will hear You."

At that moment, Miss June, who was our cook and the unofficial mother of this ministry, burst into my office without even knocking. To this day, I don't know if someone told her we were in trouble or not. But when she came in, she said, "God is fantastic!" I cannot remember how we pulled together the $2,000 we needed for that immediate crisis; but the bills were paid, the students remained, and the Enemy could not mock us.

Days passed and a prescheduled board meeting was to take place at Lacy Hayes' office. Lacy was a brilliant young attorney who was always interceding for us. I brought the board up to date with the eviction notice. Again, God's presence was preeminent. Each of the board members felt the same—they were prepared to seek God for an answer. Not one board member expressed any fear that God had forsaken us. I wanted to break into tears as several board members privately called me to reinforce their confidence in me and this work during this dark and difficult time. Someone said, "Anyone can jump ship in a crisis, but we the people of God are confident that what He began, He is able to fulfill through every adversity. We are standing with you."

The Original Board of Directors

One board member said, "I discern that somewhere inside of you, you feel you are to blame for all of these adversities, but it is not true." And he was probably right. Somewhere in my school years, my self-worth had been affected, but God was doing a new thing in me and He was using my board to confirm it.

The Fast

By the time the board convened for the next meeting, God had already begun to move among the members. Dr. Mike Innes—a well-known chiropractor and the first member of the Peniel board—demanded everyone's attention. Then he said, "God has called a three-day fast for this ministry. The stranglehold on this ministry will be defeated only through fasting and prayer."

A fast was right down Spelly's alley, and I tried to get excited about it as well . . . but my potato chips were a great comfort to me at that time, and I was wondering if I could do it. I prayed that I could bring my flesh into submission.

All the board members were extremely busy, and this time was no exception. Pastor Jerry Tow, who married Harold and me, was scheduled for a revival in Alabama. Pastor Harold Palmer, a state councilman, had an important meeting at the Church of God State Offices. Gary Altland had a large farm which required early hours and hard work . . . and the list goes on.

Mike spoke again: "All the staff and students should participate as well." I thought, *Now we've got a problem.*

"Mike," I said cautiously, "we cannot force or even suggest that our students fast for three days; government standards will not permit it. And I don't feel comfortable even asking the staff."

"I understand," Mike said. "Then, as many as will take part in this fast, let's go for it."

We never said a word to staff or students, yet they found out. Everyone except one client fasted and met us in the chapel for prayer times. It was awesome. The Spirit of the Lord was so mighty, it was as though we were in the midst of angels and walking on holy ground for those three days. The fast was completed. I made it. Thank the Lord!

We had been obedient to the Lord and had followed His instructions to the letter. The next step was to watch and wait. We fully expected the landlord's mind to change.

Imagine my surprise when I discovered our landlord was not budging. He was more difficult and as adamant as he had ever been. Dealing with this man was impossible. He was arrogant, curt, disrespectful, and was not prepared to negotiate in spite of several compromises we submitted. Proposal after counterproposal was made until it became evident that his position was final. The matter was settled.

The Power of Prayer

Spelly called the staff to prayer at a certain time every day. He told them the gravity of the situation, and they all responded the same. God had ordained this program, and they were committed to serving and trusting Him. Their response was amazing. Harry Hernandez (who later became Reverend Hernandez) was their spokesperson. He walked in a mighty anointing from God. He said the staff was not intimidated or afraid, and they would not give up anything God had ordained for His people. He declared, "The staff will stand toe-to-toe with any enemy that dares to come into the house of God and try to set up shop."

Josh Lee volunteered to speak to the students and to keep them focused. "It's serious, Mrs. Spellman," he said, "but I believe the guys will stand firm. We've got a strong bunch of men here who are not easily shaken. We will fight together."

However, the death rattles returned, louder this time. An evil spirit spoke to me, "Just give up! I have come to claim my possession. Do you not know God has forsaken you? All hope is gone. Now let me in. My name is Hopeless . . . I command you to let me in."

I remained silent as Satan taunted me night and day, indiscriminately hurling threats and accusations. He used difficult telephone calls, notices in the mail, students prematurely leaving the program, and some of the younger staff quitting. And there were the catty innuendos from some who were waiting for us to fail.

However, all was not lost. We kept reading the Word of God and claiming God's promises. We would say, as did the three Hebrew boys, "He is fully able to deliver us; but if He doesn't, we still will not bow to the enemy" (see Dan. 3:17-18).

We regained our strength, and little by little our faith was restored. God renewed our courage and empowered us with an extraordinary boldness and a deep-rooted commitment. He reminded me of the first message ever preached at Peniel by my pastor and my father in the Lord, Elder E. D. Cobbs. He preached from the Book of Esther; the theme of his message was, "If I perish, I perish; but I will do the work of the Lord." It was Bishop Cobbs who said to me, as we toured the facility that day, "Marion, I believe God is in this thing!"

That word meant everything to me. I boldly said, "My heart is fixed. Get behind me, Satan!"

Rescued From Alcoholism

One stop at a bar in 1996 ultimately became a need for a fifth every day. By 1997, I lost my job. Driving drunk with my sons in the car prompted my parents to take custody of my children. To cope with the anger and pain, I began to drink more. No matter where I was, the vodka bottle was in my hand. I lost my family, my car, my home, and my self-respect. Everything was gone.

For one and a half years, my drinking increased until one night I lay on a couch and realized I had hit rock-bottom. I cried, "Please, God, help me! I can't go on like this." I remembered my pastor telling me of a place called Peniel. Late that night, I called for help. Two weeks later, I was in the program.

During my treatment, I faced many fears, cried many tears, and went through many changes. Most important of all, Peniel is where God saved me. I learned how to live a sober life, how to take responsibility, how to cope with everyday life problems. Also, I learned how to stand and not run when things get rough. And, I was taught how to step back and look at the situation, then find a solution. In the past, my solution was another bottle of vodka; but today I can face a problem, work my way through it, and stay sober through it all!—*Angela (Georgia)*

CHAPTER 6

A RAM IN THE BUSH

We needed to move. The landlord had the nerve to raise our rent and also to ask our guys to work for him. Besides, utilities at the summer resort cost thousands of dollars, not to mention the dorm. Being a log cabin, it was still cold even with the heat being constantly increased. I later learned the potbellied stove we used was illegal, not to mention the constant flow of soot that made everything black. So, we had to go . . . but where?

At last, the breakthrough came. It happened on a Sunday evening following a service at a local church. After returning the guys to the facility, our faith-filled Miss June ran to the car from the main building.

Divine Intervention

"Wait! Wait!" she exclaimed excitedly. "I've got good news for you."

"Good news," I sighed. "What is it?" I asked, trying to share her joy.

"I found a farm for Peniel. The owners are Christians, and the daughter said the Lord told her Peniel should occupy their property."

"What!" I shouted. Now I was really excited. "What are you saying, Miss June?"

"Yes, it's time," she continued, laughing almost uncontrollably. "Isn't the Lord good?"

"I can't believe it!" I replied. "When can we see it?"

"Tomorrow. It's vacant, and we can move in any time. There are almost twelve acres!" she continued. "I saw it, and it's perfect."

Since I did not want to rain on Miss June's parade, I did all the things people do when they get good news . . . but I definitely had a hesitation. Although Spelly did not say it, I could sense a "slow-down spirit" on him as well. I thought, *I hope Miss June doesn't sense his caution; she will be crushed.* We had good reason to be guarded. In this short time of ministry, we had learned nothing is *ever* totally free. Everything has a price tag. We had also learned things that appear to be too good to be true probably are. And I learned the hard way that not all free things necessarily come from God. But I hid the uncertainty in my heart, eager to receive the details.

"Praise the Lord!" I said with as much joy as I could muster.

My mother, who was visiting us from Pittsburgh, interrupted: "God is so good! I knew He wouldn't fail us. It only seems reasonable that He would open this door for Peniel. God wants to rescue lives in this last day, and He is using Peniel to accomplish His purpose. All you kids need to do is provide the sinners; He will provide the Savior and meet every need." She insisted, "Remember, I told you kids to put your trust in the Lord. Hallelujah! Harold, didn't I tell you?"

Well, I thought, *Momma's on board. That's a good sign.*

"Yes, Mom," Spelly said, laughing. "You're right, as usual." Then, looking at me, he winked and said, "Babe, did we bring a lunch? I think Momma is about to preach." (If you knew how shy my mother was at public speaking, you would get the joke.)

"Sounds like it to me," I said, pretending she couldn't hear us.

"OK," Mom said. "All I have to say is my God has come through again, just as I said He would!"

We rejoiced all the way home, trying to keep Momma's faith alive, but both of us knew the dangers that lay ahead if they were indeed saying this was a free farm. We had visited the free arena years earlier when Peniel was just a seed in my heart. Someone from Harrisburg had given us a house. I was sure it was from God, and I believed it was a sign that God wanted us to start this ministry. We were given exaggerated details of the house, and we had accepted it sight unseen. We were going to use this house for the Lord!

However, I had not asked the Lord if He even wanted it! I found out after I got this dilapidated, falling-apart structure that God had not sent these people to give this to us. More than that, God didn't even want this place! I couldn't use it . . . I couldn't sell it . . . God did not want it . . . and I couldn't give it away! It was uninhabitable. Mold had overtaken this place. I don't remember how long God let us sweat it out, but it seemed like forever. Finally, the township bulldozed that entire row of houses as I shouted, "Hallelujah. Glory to God!"

Now I am an "expert" on free gifts! I know that when a gift seems appealing, it is vital to see if God sent the person and if He wants to use what they are bringing. If God does not sanction the deal, count me out! I was now thinking like Moses when he said to God, "Here is the deal. Lord, if You don't go with us, I'm just not goin'!" (the Spellman version of Ex. 33:15).

When the day came to see the property, I was eager. Our staff was excited as well. "Your appointment to see the property is at 9 o'clock this morning," Becki said as I walked in the door.

"Appointment?" I questioned. "What appointment?"

"To see the farm!" she replied.

"Oh, I forgot," I said facetiously.

“Sure, sure,” she answered, laughing heartily.

“Seriously,” I said. “How does the rest of the day look?”

“I kept it clear for you ’cause I didn’t know how much time you would need to inspect the property.”

“Good girl,” I said, winking at her. After giving the staff instructions for the day, Harold and I were off to see the property.

After a telephone call to confirm the meeting, Spelly and I headed for the Sawyer Ranch in York, Pennsylvania. The conversation between us was guarded. Neither one of us wanted to speak anything negative into the situation. The owners had relocated to Kentucky and had appointed their daughter, Terry, to negotiate on their behalf. Miss June knew the family and had influenced the daughter to be an advocate for Peniel.

We finally arrived. The ranch was situated in a small, quaint part of town. It really was lovely. The ranch sat on a fourteen-acre manicured lawn with a couple of buildings—a huge, well-kept barn and a house. The house had several bedrooms, a comfortable dining room, and a medium-sized kitchen equipped with a lovely fireplace. As we walked through, I wondered how we could make this work. The facility itself was so beautiful that our overwhelming desire was to make it work.

“Yes,” I said to Terry, “yes, this will work.” All the time I was thinking, *How in the world would we make it a reality?* Spelly jumped in. “Do you think your parents will allow us to convert the barn into a dormitory?” he asked.

“I don’t know,” she replied, “but I will ask them tonight when I call them.”

“If we can do that, we can make the house into our offices and make it work,” he said.

Yes, I thought! *That is exactly right*! We made a little more small conversation and agreed to await her call after speaking to her parents.

The next morning, Terry called. “My parents want to know if you will drive down to Kentucky for a face-to-face meeting.”

Without even asking Spelly, I promptly replied, "Yes; when?"

"At your convenience," she replied.

I promised to get back to her with details and hung up. "Spelly," I said, "her parents want a face-to-face meeting in Kentucky."

"OK," he said, "when do we leave?"

I gave him a kiss and said, "I knew you would say that. If Becki will stay with Daddy and Skip [our son], we can leave tomorrow." Becki agreed.

We made the arrangements, got the directions, and headed for Kentucky. The Sawyers were waiting for us when we drove down their long, gorgeous driveway. We met, and it was as though we had known them for years. They were warm, kind, and ready to help us. This actually turned into a mini-vacation. They had heard about Peniel before leaving for Kentucky and were on board.

We agreed on the rent and they agreed on us turning the barn into a dorm. We did not haggle—God was in this. After the business was over, they encouraged us to stay a couple of days longer, and we did. It was wonderful. There was a great peace in their home.

Meeting the Sawyers

Finally, it was time to go. Spelly hugged Mrs. Sawyer and kissed her on the cheek. Thanking them on our behalf, he spoke a blessing on their home. As they stood on the porch seeing us off, I did not want to look back because I hated leaving them. They truly were representing the Lord, and I was thankful for the opportunity to spend that time with them.

As we talked about the trip on the way home, I felt strange. Everything had gone so smoothly! *When is the other shoe going to drop*? I wondered, but dared not say it. Spelly didn't "play" regarding blessings and worrying about a pending problem. He would surely give me a long sermon on "In all things, be thankful." So I sat back and enjoyed the great blessing!

The Sawyer Property

Invitation to the Brouhaha

The owner of Dillsburg agreed for the guys to stay until we could renovate the barn . . . if we could do this in the allotted time. Now it was time to move what we could and take possession of the property while simultaneously applying for an occupancy permit.

During the process of filing the application, we were told the barn, which was 10 feet from the road, had to be 100 feet away. We were summoned to a township meeting to plead our case.

We knew we needed legal counsel, so we contacted attorney Russell Albert, a member of our board of directors. Russell was on the legal staff in the office of Governor Dick Thornburgh. Because of his position, he was unable to represent us in a township dispute because he felt it might be viewed as a conflict of interest. However, he recommended Lacy Hayes.

Lacy was a young Christian attorney who was community-minded, extremely smart, and most importantly, anointed by the Lord. Day after day, we were facing inciting headlines in the papers prior to the township meeting. Finally, the evening arrived. The meeting was scheduled for 7 p.m. We arrived at 6:45. The town hall was so crowded and noisy that we could hardly get in. Finally, we were inside where they had saved a seat for us. We were ushered to the front of the building. People were standing outside yelling, "No drug program here—not in our community! It will never open—never!"

It was difficult for the chairperson to bring order in the room. Even when he threatened to throw out violators, we could still hear an undercurrent. Every point the chairperson made, the audience would either clap or sigh. Lacy sat quietly as they stated their case. Finally, it was his turn to speak. Lacy slowly rose to his feet and opened his comments with these words: "We did not come to fight; we have come here tonight in the name of the Lord." He said these words with such an anointing that a holy hush covered the room. It was awesome. He then began to present our case in a respectful manner.

After he concluded, the room was blanketed by a spirit of respect and self-control. With that, the town leaders determined we could operate Peniel on this property, but we would have to move the barn back 100 feet to meet stipulations. It was the law. On our way out, several people tapped Spelly and Lacy on their backs as if to say, *I am sorry; I didn't understand.*

These same people were now actually thanking us for coming. Another miracle!

My Transformed Life

I am thankful for all God has done for me. A little over four years ago, my life was in complete chaos. After struggling with an addiction to drugs and alcohol for more than twenty-five years, I realized I had to make a drastic change. After destroying many relationships and breaking the hearts of many family members, I was ready to surrender. I am thankful to my sister who told me about Peniel—where, if I was willing, I could begin the process of restoration.

First, I rededicated my life back to God. The classes, the one-on-one counseling, the group sessions, and chapel services all worked together to restore me. There were moments of despair, guilt, and loneliness; however, God was able, with the help of the great staff at Peniel, to bring me through. Life is enriching as I speak into the lives of others who are overcoming the things I was delivered from. I am eternally grateful to God and the staff at Peniel for my transformed life.—*Kim*

CHAPTER 7

CAMP SERTOMA

We were on our way home following the difficult meeting with the York Township supervisors. After realizing his passion for the ministry and having represented us so well, Lacy Hayes was asked to become a member of our board of directors. He told us he was also on the board of Camp Sertoma in Lingelstown, Pennsylvania, which was conveniently located near Peniel. This organization did a tremendous work serving physically and mentally challenged children.

Lacy mentioned the camp was not presently in use since they always closed for the winter. Nevertheless, he offered to ask them if they would allow the Peniel students to stay there; but he stressed this was only a "Band-Aid." We would need to quickly decide what our next step would be because this facility was not insulated, so it would not be an option for the winter months.

Their board of directors agreed, but only on the condition that at the first sign of a temperature drop, we would move out immediately. Lacy went on to say that Camp Sertoma's maintenance people were "on the ready" to come in and winterize the facility.

We are talking about big-time pressure! Still, we assured him we would indeed meet this condition.

Another Miracle

Incredibly, the winter weather made headlines in Harrisburg, Pennsylvania, that year. Newspapers and newscasters alike commented daily about the unseasonably warm weather. Our students were walking around in short pants in November and December. Another miracle!

Spelly, along with the male staff, and the students were at Sertoma, while Miss June, Becki, Marion Shultz, and I worked about fifty miles away at the Sawyers' ranch. I ran the administration while Spelly ran the program, and God kept His word.

I often tell people what Bishop Roland Vaughan profoundly said in a message he preached to the Peniel congregation: "I would rather go to war with a soldier who has scars than with a soldier who has open wounds. The scars indicate he has healed from his wounds, while open wounds reveal the area is still raw and capable of infecting others."

When the way seems dark and every door to victory is closed, there are five things we can do until our change comes.

1. *Devour God's Word.* Your desire should be to know God intimately. This relationship is to have absolutely no conditions to sustain it. Whether your dreams materialize or not has nothing to do with your relationship with God. Do the right thing because it is the right thing to do.

2. *Get a "Spelly" in your life.* You need someone who will not compromise God's Word—like Harold Spellman has done in my life—even if you have to run on "empty" for a while. Too often we are unable to discern if we should take a stand with God that might put us at odds with our neighbors, or if we should offer genuine compassion to them, which will provide the comfort they desperately need. Either way, we must never allow a soldier to cry alone.

3. *Pray as if everything depends on God, and work as if everything depends on you.* This principle, coined by Augustine, is an absolute in the work of God. Faith does not mean there is nothing for you to do. God will not move until you have done all you know to do. God helps us to present a balance in this world. Every miracle God has supplied for Peniel happened when we first had done all we knew to do. Just as we should not live from paycheck to paycheck, we do not live from miracle to miracle.

4. *Whistle while you work.* In other words, maintain a song in your heart. It is easy to sink into depression and unknowingly display poor interaction skills. We must guard our hearts against hurt feelings, unforgiveness, and jealousy. Don't buy the lie that because you are silent, you have not offended your brother. Silence can be as powerful as rage. People can be severely punished without a word being spoken. I have found it is impossible to negatively react to disappointments if there is a song in your heart and you get busy singing it out. It's OK if you do not have a beautiful voice; at some point your song will shift into a prayer of thanksgiving anyway.

5. *Give*! Give out of your need, but do not give at the risk of failing to pay your bills or feeding your family. We are commanded to take care of our responsibilities, but too often the need is so great in our lives that we do not dare give some of what we have. I believe in sacrificial giving, and that such giving will not bring a reproach on you, your family, or your God.

Spiritual Growth

Camp Sertoma was a tremendous blessing to Peniel. In that facility, the residents enjoyed many conveniences that were not available to us before.

The camp was set back in the scenic Pennsylvania mountains, almost as though a special place was prepared just for us. Eleven cabins comfortably accommodated four guys per room. The commercial kitchen was fully equipped. There was

Camp Sertoma

also a large cafeteria. The recreational buildings were converted into classrooms, and other rooms were used as makeshift offices. We decided to utilize the pay phone that was already in operation, rather than incur the expense of installing a new system for such a short period of time.

The live-in staff readily accepted our new situation with gratitude, even though the property was isolated. The three months we were housed at Camp Sertoma could have easily seemed to be a hardship to the staff, but instead they used the opportunity to study the Word of God, pray, and fast.

In retrospect, I attribute our stability and spiritual growth during that time directly to the Peniel staff members, who found a deeper place in God. God taught the students and the staff great lessons that can only be appreciated when experienced.

This different situation inspired Robert Cox, who was one of our most conscientious counselors. He rarely became involved with the administrative part of Peniel; rather, he worked diligently to perfect his skills as a counselor.

Working late into the night, he would reason with the guys concerning the value of their souls and God's eternal plan for their lives. His treatment plans were an expression of Brother Cox's greatest desire, which was to bring his counselees to a face-to-face encounter with the Lord.

Brother Cox's "down time" was spent in libraries researching other Christian materials—always in search of a more effective approach. Taking out his handkerchief to wipe his eyes, Brother Cox once said to me, "I really don't know all that is happening with the ministry, but I want you to know I am praying, and I know God is greater than any problem we are facing." He was obviously moved by the Spirit of God to speak to me.

"I know, Brother Cox," I said gently. "Thanks for sharing that with me. We are going to make it."

"I have no doubt," he continued, "not even one."

Four Encouraging Words

For a moment, I felt responsible for making this whole thing work. It was overwhelming to think about it. Some staff members changed their whole lifestyles; others chose to relocate; many were willing to face the financial challenges—all because of their strong belief God had called Peniel into existence and He had called them to be a part of this great work.

Considering the adversities we had already faced, it could have been easy for someone to question if God was in this endeavor. I was the voice He used to call it into being. I was so sure I had been given the plan for how God wanted me to oversee this program. Four words resounded in my heart: *respect, protect, direct,* and *inspect*. Those basic principles were non-negotiable, as far as I understood them.

Over and over I would say to the staff, "It won't be long. God's getting ready to bless us. I can feel it." But was I only trying to convince myself? I'd prefer to believe that I was doing as David did when he commanded his soul to "boast in the Lord" (Ps. 34:2).

Back at the Ranch

Fifty miles away at the Sawyer Ranch, Becki, Marion Shultz, and I were running the administration. Miss June was busy developing menus and culinary policies. Meanwhile, the bills were coming in from two facilities. One of our immediate concerns was our phone bill—we had an invoice we could not pay. Spelly's response to the problem was, "If God doesn't send the money in, then He wants us to continue functioning without a phone."

"Without a phone!" I responded, aggravated with him. Looking me right in the eyes, he emphatically replied, "Without a phone!"

I stomped out of the room, declaring his insanity. "He can't be serious" I protested. There was no point in talking to him about it. The word *quit* is not in the man's vocabulary. As far as he was concerned, the tools we were given were the tools we would use . . . even if there were no tools.

I went back to my office and tried to calm down. I asked Becki if I had all of the receipts, hoping she would say there were some that I had not yet received.

"Yes, Ma'am, they are all there."

Halfheartedly, I began to punch in the figures. *Wow!* I thought. *This is more than I had on the deposit slips before me. Let me do it again.* A nervousness began to churn in my stomach. Would God repeat the miracle He had done before? I called for Becki. We took turns, as we had done before. We slowly called the numbers out to each other . . . and the totals continued to increase. We were sitting in the middle of another miracle!

God had once again increased the "oil in our jars" (see 2 Kings 4:1-7). We were able to pay our creditors . . . with "oil" to spare. Spelly, Becki, and I will *never* forget these miracles. But it was not enough for us to stay in that place. I knew we could not live on miracles. We still were facing the urgency to move.

Homeless Again

Because people did not understand the value of what we were trying to do, we were facing homelessness again. The message was clear and precise. Just as we had been asked to vacate our previous facility, now this township was echoing the same sentiments. We felt like wandering sheep without a home or shepherd.

Hoping to find a loophole, I would periodically reread the eviction notice, and then I would read the township's stipulations again. Maybe we had missed something, or perhaps someone was playing an ugly joke. But it wasn't a joke, bad or otherwise. The program was really facing the possibility of closing.

Panic struck my heart. What in the world could we do with all these guys, not to mention the wives and children with whom we were working?

Through it all, my husband exhibited a supernatural calmness, so much so that it angered me. I wanted him to fret and worry like I was, but he refused to do so. He insisted on reinforcing his faith and would not yield to frustration, worry, or doubt. He was difficult to live with . . . or maybe it was me who needed to refocus.

Still, the situation looked so bad that I thought no one on our board would support a decision for the program to continue. Certainly the businessmen—known to respond only to the bottom line, whether red or black—would be ready to throw in the towel.

However, these were truly men of God who had accomplished great things in their own ministries. These were the same men who fasted and prayed to defeat a previous giant! They would not be deterred by adversity.

"Yes!" I said to myself, "*Focus!* Keep a stiff upper lip; stir up your confidence, girl, and don't you dare give in to your fears, but hold on to your faith!"

We were all working under pressure, but it was obvious the Lord was working something out in our lives. It was not just the concern of dealing with overdue bills—it was one problem after another, day after day. I was afraid to answer the phone, so maybe Spelly was right—maybe we didn't need it after all. I felt like I was drowning. It hurt so badly, but in my heart I knew I'd rather bear my cross in the work of the Lord than to enjoy the greatest pleasure I had without Christ in the world.

Anointed With Oil

Later at home, as I silently stood over the sink with tears running down my cheek, Harold said softly, "Babe, we have chosen Jesus above everything! If our situation changes, then thank God. But if it doesn't change, it does not mean God has changed His mind; He is just leading us another way. He has never failed us, and He never will."

He added, "Let me pray for you. Where is the anointing oil?"

"It's in the bedroom, I think," I said, barely looking around the room.

"Oh, here it is," he said. Then, taking the oil, Harold gently anointed my forehead. Again, we entered the presence of the Lord together. He carefully laid out the graveness of the situations we were facing, methodically reminding God of each challenge for which we had no answer, and closed his prayer with a reminder that this ministry belonged to Him.

My dear friend, Dr. Barbara M. Amos, has taught me so much about going before the Lord. She has the attitude that when she lays her petitions before Him, she is careful to make it clear to Him she is not *complaining*—she is just *explaining*.

"I feel good!" Harold said with a confidence that I knew was real. Then he pinched me gently and continued, "I'm looking for something wonderful to happen—maybe tonight!"

I shook my head, trying to convey to my husband that he was on the borderline of being ridiculous! After all, it was normal to worry a little . . . wasn't it?

"You can worry and fret if you want," he said, noticing my signal but ignoring its implications, "but I choose to believe the Lord!" With that, he went into the living room, and suddenly tackled Skip, throwing him onto the floor.

A Lesson From Skip

As I saw them wrestling on the floor, I first became angry. This was no time to play. We were in trouble. Could anybody hear me?

But as I silently watched, I could hear the hearty laughter of Skip as his dad demanded him to acknowledge his strength and submit to the "super-duper" hold that his father had on him.

"Submit, submit!" his dad repeated with authority.

"No, no, I won't! I won't!" Skip kept saying.

Finally, Skip managed to get to his feet. Then they came barreling out of the living room, whizzing past me through the kitchen and into the pantry.

"Harold . . . Skip!" I said sternly. "You guys better stop it before you break something!"

"Mom, Mom!" Skip said, trying to stop laughing long enough to express his thoughts. "You'd better take him off me . . . before I hurt him."

What was he saying? His dad was definitely in control of the entire situation, but in Skip's mind, he did not acknowledge the obvious; rather, he spoke according to his faith. In Skip's mind, he had not used all of his resources yet. He saw himself as the victor.

Skip's persevering spirit became highly contagious. Suddenly, I became aware of the great lesson the Lord was using our son to teach us. *Submitting was not the answer!* The matter was settled—we would continue to wait on the Lord, because He is our help and our strength. Indeed, He is our champion. Just as Skip had somehow managed to get to his feet, so would Peniel.

By this, I was renewed and refreshed. We would receive our answer . . . maybe even tonight!

Love and Respect

I am fifty-six years old, and I never thought of myself as a bad person. I always kept a job, but I really didn't have it together. I couldn't do anything unless I was high, and once I got high, nothing got done! Bills piled up, and I missed my children's special events.

Thank God for my pastor who saw through all of my deceit and told me about Peniel. He said, "Your life can be restored, and you can be the man that God planned for you to be." I wanted to be that man.

On September 12, 2001, I arrived at Peniel. One of the most valued lessons they taught me was that when you're treated with love and respect, you can love and respect others. The program isn't easy, but it's the best program for people like me whose lives are broken and who don't know where to turn. I am forever grateful for Peniel. There I found out who I was, to whom I belong, and where my place is.

Thirteen years later, I have a true sense of direction. I have a loving wife who puts God before me, and children and grandchildren who now follow our example.—*Frank*

CHAPTER 8

OUR PROMISED LAND

With the help of our board of directors, we were able to find a wonderful place in York Springs that we would soon call home. We were working against the clock since we knew if the temperatures dropped, we would have to immediately vacate the premises at Camp Sertoma where the students were temporarily staying.

The place we were looking at was so beautiful, I could hardly believe it! This was a neat and well-kept, very large farmhouse located on sixty-three acres in the middle of one-hundred thousand acres of fruit orchards. It was a greater blessing than I had ever dreamed. The farmhouse was situated along a quiet, tree-lined road, yet it was easily accessible to the city. The interior could be transformed easily to meet our needs. The hardwood floors sparkled. Each of the rooms was constructed in a way that could be adapted easily. This would serve as our administration building.

There was a large dining room, but not quite large enough. *No problem*, I thought. *We will have to start serving the meals earlier and just schedule them according to the client phases.*

York Springs Facility

The spacious grounds would provide enough area for our guys to experience God's undisturbed beauty during their recreational and vocational times. There was also a huge storage building that could accommodate fifty guys. Beneath it was a very large and immaculate building that was formerly used to crate apples, which would later become our chapel. It would be a place where numerous men and their families would meet the Savior, like the shepherds who found the Christ child in a manger.

As we toured, I said, "This is perfect!"

Spelly said, "I think you're right."

"Do you really think it will work?" I asked.

"I think so, but let's slow down for a minute."

"Thanks," I said. "Let's slow it down. We need to call Bill Derrick." Bill was a member of our board and also our realtor. "Let's see what he says."

We immediately telephoned Bill, told him we had gone to see this farm, and asked him what he thought about it. He looked up the property from his office and said it was a good possibility.

Bill provided us with the details of the property within three days. "I've gone over the stats carefully," he said, "and I'm thinking it can be done."

A meeting was scheduled at Bill's office. I sat there with my heart in my throat. The preliminaries seemed endless, and the spirit of this meeting felt entirely too casual. What was this laughing and joking about? I didn't want people to be congenial or even cordial to each other. *Let's get right to the problem. We're in a crisis.*

Oh yes, I smiled politely and laughed in the right places, as best as I could, but I was in pure agony. Peniel was in a jam—we were homeless! We had fifty students with nowhere to go! Did these guys on this board not get it?

Finally, the pending situation was opened for discussion. It makes me tremble when I tell you what happened next. The atmosphere did not change, but God certainly changed the situation.

A man named Alan Bittner, who was not a board member, was at this meeting. He was a devout Christian who testified that one day he was looking out of his window and saw me crossing the street. The Lord spoke to his heart, "Go help that lady."

Alan owned a used-car business. We did not know each other before he approached me, but he honored what God had said to him; in fact, he had recently given Becki a Volkswagen. He testified in one of the church services that when his business was in a slump, he would give Peniel a car or van and then he would sell cars like crazy!

I do not know who had invited Alan to this board meeting; but as he leaned back in his chair, he quietly looked on the wall where Bill had various properties posted, and picked out the farm we were to discuss. Alan calmly said, "This is the place. God has given us this place."

Spelly, Bill, and I were amazed! We did not have to convince anyone about this farm. The matter was settled. This would be our new home. Now we had to convince the owner to sell it to us.

Our income was sporadic and unstable. We all knew it, but no one voiced it. Instead, we developed a plan to show our confidence in this ship that everyone thought was sinking.

Here was our strategy: Spelly and I would put on our very best. We would be well dressed, but not overdressed. Bill would use his car, which was a brand-new Lincoln. We would be interested, but not overly eager. Bill, the realtor, would do all the talking and we would walk through the house, nodding our heads in the appropriate places. Bill had run the background on the property, and he knew the owners were in the middle of a divorce and therefore eager to sell. We would not make a commitment at that time; in fact, we would tell them we were going to look at other properties (and we did—we made sure to look at them on the wall in Bill's office).

The plan worked. Through God's hand, Spelly and the owner bonded. They grew to like each other, and they still have a good relationship. The negotiations took on the usual back and forth until we agreed on the purchase conditions. We would purchase this new property based on the tax write-off the owner agreed to accept. The monthly payments were reasonable, but reasonable was never the question; attainable was the villain lurking in every corner with a key in his hand. Thank God it was only a key—not the key. Praise God, the deal was done! The property was ours.

The New Dormitory and New York

Relaxing as we drove back home, Becki said, "Don't forget, you have an appointment with Basil and Josh to discuss the plumbing."

"Oh, yes," I said. "Thank the Lord for them; they are truly lifesavers."

When we approached them regarding the problems of the new facility, they said, "Yes, we can install the bathrooms. Let us know when you are ready to begin and have a couple of guys to help."

As the plumbing work began, the property began to take on a new identity. Now the dormitory was almost ready for occupancy. It was beautiful to behold the God-given abilities of so many people working together to accomplish a common goal.

This was a new day presenting new opportunities. With all that was going on, Peniel received an invitation to spend a week in New York. This assignment would be a labor of love, making an investment in hurting lives. Members of the Peniel staff would work closely with the six liaison pastors from that area.

"Honey," Spelly said, fearing we might cancel the trip because of finances, "the harvest is very ripe in New York. There are so many young people who need to hear the gospel—kids who live on the same streets where I used to hustle. The pastors from New York who volunteered to help us are real men of God. I know them personally. They are sympathetic to this type of program, and their hearts break for those who abuse drugs and alcohol. I am sure these pastors will welcome any we may win into their churches. They will have a great influence on them."

Even though I had concerns regarding the expenses involved for the trip to New York, we decided to go. I chose not to discuss finances with Josh except to caution him about spending wisely and to document every purchase, which is our established policy anyway.

"Call me every day," I said, finally making known the decision in the matter. "And may the Lord bless you, Greg, and Lewis, with an abundant harvest."

Just as Harry Hernandez had predicted, the trip was an overwhelming success . . . and as I had feared, we took a sizable financial hit. However, the monetary loss was less important and became obscure in contrast to the eternal work these men had accomplished by our obedience. Reports continued to pour in from New York for a long time.

The encouraging feedback received from those street meetings indicated that several churches received new members and many unchurched families heard the gospel for the first time. People attending those meetings were made aware of concerned congregations in their area who were willing to intercede on their behalf as ambassadors for Christ. In addition, young addicts were enrolled in the Peniel drug program and taught God's plan for their lives. Two brothers from New York who had abused drugs for years and had been in and out of trouble were admitted to Peniel, and the positive results greatly affected their family. Only eternity will reveal the total impact of Peniel's trip to New York.

The Move

At last, the drama that seemed to always find its way to our doors was finally coming to an end. It was time to transport the guys to our new home. "The best way to do this," I told the staff, "is to get organized. Everyone must have an assignment and be accountable to a supervisor for carrying out his or her particular job."

Then I told Miss June, "You will be in charge of the kitchen and dining area. You will need about three or four guys to help you. Be careful to take only those items that belong to Peniel. The other items in the kitchen are to be washed and neatly stacked for an easy inventory by the Camp Sertoma staff."

Next, I told Becki and Marion Shultz, "Pack everything in your department except the equipment needed to maintain the daily routine. Ladies, you will be in charge of all the offices. I will assign four junior staff members to assist you. We will continue to observe the established rules!"

"Gotcha," Marion said, taking notes of the meeting.

"Now, Mike, you will supervise moving the guys' personal belongings and cleaning the dorm. Each student will be responsible for packing his own belongings. After that job is completed, work as a team to get the dorm shipshape. It is important, Mike, to make sure none of the guys' personal belongings are lost. Their things are valuable to them."

"Right!" Mike agreed. "I'll be careful."

Spelly interrupted, "I'll take a few guys over to the new property and begin the cleanup there while you guys work here."

"Great idea, Honey! Is there anything I've forgotten?" I asked.

Spelly paused for a moment and began laughing with the staff. Then he said, "Only the cars, the blessing room, the utility room, the shed, the garage, and—"

"Ok-a-a-ay, okay," I giggled. "I get the message."

"Just leave it to me, Babe," he said. "You take care of the paperwork, and I'll do the rest."

I knew he was right to take charge of the move. His plan would cause less confusion. Harold and I had agreed on the most efficient way to run the program: I would work in administration while he worked with the guys. God seemed to use us best this way.

At that time, Harold was the *heavy* around the center. He did the chastening and the dismissing of unruly clients. He is strict, but full of compassion; easily touched and quick to forgive. He has a deep love for the male staff and an obvious respect for the women who labor with us.

Yes, without a doubt, God's plan for Peniel is to run a tight ship, and Harold can carry out that plan. Together, Harold and I have adopted guidelines and a code of ethics from the Word of God, and we endeavor to meet those standards.

"This program is built on God's Word," Harold has been heard to say. "And when we no longer abide by it, count me out."

The move was an experience I shall never forget. While God made this great provision, He did not wave a magic wand and . . . *abracadabra* . . . we were all moved. On the contrary, the move was difficult and required hard work by everyone.

Think about moving a large family. Now multiply that by 50. Add a complete toolshed, a large blessing room, an operating garage, plus an extensive library. Throw in a large pantry full of food and six rooms of heavy office furniture. Finally, include loads of wood for construction. Don't forget the building filled with appliances.

Also, remember the vehicles, particularly those that had to be towed. Did I neglect to mention the fun we had moving the large pianos? Enough of that talk; it's exhausting just thinking about it.

The staff and residents probably worked as hard as they had ever worked in their lives. Still, there was a *sweet, sweet* spirit abiding within Peniel. It was precious how the Holy Spirit inspired our residents to praise Him during this time. All over the property we could hear the guys singing, "We're free to be the servants of the Lord."

Our "Exodus"

As we observed the residents and staff filing down the path from the dorm to load the trucks, Harold said, "This scene reminds me of the children of Israel as they prepared to leave Egypt."

"Oh, yes! Honey, that's right," I replied. "Look at those with boxes on their heads and others with clothes under their arms. The only thing missing is the jewels they took from the Egyptians, huh?"

"I've got my 'jewel' right here beside me," Harold said with a twinkle in his eye.

Praise the Lord, not one incident was reported during the entire move. When the job was finally completed, we knew a time of dedication and thankfulness was in order. It was obvious that our great God had made this provision for us. Further, He had prevented Satan's relentless attack to put us to an open shame by destroying this ministry.

The Dedication

After moving in, the first thing on the agenda was to dedicate our new property to the Lord. Gathering the staff and residents, a large caravan of thankful Christians headed for the new center. I wish you could have been there. It was an incredible, awesome day of celebrating the greatness of our God! The dedication service was held during our regularly scheduled chapel. The air was filled with songs, testimonies, and high praise to our magnificent God who had defended us and conquered our Enemy.

The Lord blessed us by sending Bishop Jerry Tow to officiate during the service. He and his lovely wife, Leaha, were Spelly's and my wonderful pastors and personal friends. Jerry also was the one who married us. Pastor Tow believed in Peniel when it was not the popular thing to do. The guys adored him because he refused to label them; instead, he saw them as hungry souls needing God's Word. With the busy schedule of a pastor, somehow he found time to preach in our chapel periodically without receiving any financial remuneration. Yes, it was only fitting that God chose this special man to do the honors.

We all gathered in our makeshift chapel, but because of the pelting rain that day, the staff saw very little of the actual property. Still in our hearts, the "Son" was brightly shining.

The Plaque

The staff found humor in almost everything. For instance, because they had worked extremely hard during the move and wanted Spelly and me to know it, one morning I found an impressive package on my desk. Inside was a plaque that had a picture of a funny-looking gorilla with the inscription, "Don't bother me—I'm having a crisis." No one claimed to have sent it, but we all had a great laugh.

Another time, the staff and students bought us a set of luggage for a surprise party. The only problem was finding a date for the party without us knowing about it. Every time it was scheduled, we were not available because of previous commitments. As a last resort, we were given the luggage during a chapel service . . . without the party. We laughed because everyone knows how I love surprises—especially those with presents.

God Has a Plan

In 1988 I started using drugs. What began as fun led to an obsession I could not control. I abused my wife, family, and friends. Slowly, I watched my life go up in smoke. Finally, in October 1999, after eleven years of a life of hell, I went to Peniel.

My plan was to run away from my problems again until everything blew over. But God—the One from whom I had been running for years—still had a plan for my life. I told my counselor, "You don't understand—I have done too much; I have gone too far."

Mr. Henry simply said, "David, it's OK; I've been there too. God can do anything." This attitude in the staff showed me who God really is.

Thank God, His plans are bigger than my plans! Through the classes, chapel, and just watching men like Pastor Spellman and my counselor, Mr. Henry, God taught me how to live as a true man of God.—*David (Alabama)*

CHAPTER 9

ALL THINGS WORK TOGETHER

We may have lived under constant financial pressures, but I felt secure about the staff. People would often comment on the wonderful staff God had called to work at Peniel.

We started with twenty-six people who answered the call. We had more staff than we had clients. It was amazing! We would often discuss that ministry had dual purposes in our lives. It was as much for the staff as it was for the client. Everyone would nod in agreement with an assurance about the blessing of being called to serve.

Blessing the Staff

All of the staff knew the financial condition of Peniel before they came aboard. Their compensation was discussed, and staff members were given time to determine if they would be able to live with the amount that Peniel was able to provide. Nearly every staff member had supplemental income, and those who did not were able to get churches or individuals to consider them as missionaries with monthly financial support.

As often as possible, I approved assistance for staff members in immediate need. My goal was to demonstrate they were as important as the students. We would share excess food and other donated supplies. I asked individuals who made donations, "Do you mind if I share a portion of this with the staff? This will be such a blessing."

"Yes," they would invariably say. "It is up to you to use wherever you decide."

We would often brag on how faithful God was and how He was able to take care of what belonged to Him. What a blessing it was to raise up churches and people to care for the staff. Still today, I respond in my letters of appreciation, "Thank you for passing the ammunition!" The staff is always so grateful for the extra blessings!

The Plan

Staff members had homes, cars, and food. Many were able to have savings accounts as well. I believed someday God would provide the benefits of which the staff was certainly worthy. The plan I felt the Lord had given to me was for the Peniel facility to effectively compete with secular programs and establish the respect of the professional world, producing individuals who had been completely delivered and responsible to society. We could then approach the appropriate agencies and develop an in-house program that would make the program self-sustaining.

Certainly we were eligible and qualified for the grants that colleges and other human-service agencies receive. My mentors were institutions like Lee University and Pathway Press, where pioneers had been called with little compensation until God opened the financial doors. We, the founders of Peniel, were called to lay a foundation that many would later reap in this world; our labor would not be in vain. I believed we were investing in God's eternal rewards.

The Mutiny

I had no idea what was brewing at the pool. Miss June, Becki, and I had been kept out of the loop. No one knew that I was about to have one of the most devastating meetings ever.

There was a knock on my door, and about a dozen staff members walked in together. As I looked up, something within me thought, *This is not good.* Someone immediately said, "We have come to hand in our resignations."

Of course, I was speechless! A lump arose in my stomach. "What happened?" I finally managed to ask.

"We discussed this among ourselves, and we've also been praying."

"What are you saying? What happened?" was all I could manage to say.

They then identified the person among them who suggested they pray about me, and for a while, they had been meeting at the pool praying for me. After much prayer and discussion, they had decided God was no longer directing me.

"I have to accept your decision," I said, trying not to break into tears, "but why did you have these meetings in secret? You have received a wrong report. God is still with us, but if it is time for you to move on, I have to hear you. Still, I am concerned about the way this whole thing was done."

One by one, they filed by and laid their resignations on my desk.

I called a dear friend and broke into tears. All I could say was, "I am having staff problems." I had decided I would not be specific. Calling her was not a good idea—I actually felt worse after the conversation! My friend began to question why I was so depressed. Did I not know that many trials and disappointments were going to come? She went on, insinuating that if I were a stronger Christian, I would just roll with the punches.

I was so glad when that conversation was over! All I could do was sit and look out the window.

Maybe they were right! What did God want from me? How much can someone be expected to take? Where was God? Why wasn't He on my side? How could He see them working against me and let this happen? Why didn't they include Miss June? She would have put them right!

I needed to add my resignation to the pile and be done with it. Surely, I didn't need this! There were other things I could do.

Regrouping

Becki, Miss June, and I never discussed the incident. Did they even know? Becki had not relocated to Harrisburg yet, so she might not even have known what was happening. And I was too hurt, angry, and crushed to talk about it. Instead, I used "smart mouthing" as a defense mechanism, but I longed to make things right with the resigning staff. I was so sorry it had come to this. Now there wasn't any male staff, and we had thirty guys in the dorms. *What should I do? God . . . what should I do?*

"Mom" June

I called in four of the oldest, most stable clients and laid it out on the table. Then I told them we were without male staff for now, and we had two options: we could relocate the house to another facility, or they could help me oversee the house until we could work through this situation.

"Don't worry; we've got your back," they said in unison. "We will help you with the program, and we will maintain the schedule just as everything is posted." *Had they overheard my telephone call to my friend, and was God telling me, through these clients, to be encouraged?*

Feeling a tear in the corner of my eyes and clearing my voice, I said with as much confidence that I was able to muster, "Thanks, guys! Help me by not discussing this situation in the dorm. Mr. Spellman will be your supervisor and will be meeting with you and the rest of the guys regularly for the counseling sessions. Miss June and I will join Mr. Spellman in conducting the classes."

Well, we all pulled together! It was not as bad as my nightmares threatened. Incidents were reported and promptly addressed. All were where they were supposed to be, when they were supposed to be there. We did not have a serious infraction during this time; and here is the best news—a large percentage of that class is still serving God in significant positions today.

The Cleansing

God can turn lemons into lemonade. This crisis gave God the platform to identify true leaders in that class we would never have seen otherwise. There were teachers and even preachers among us, and we knew it not! Students took a stand for what was right—they would not tolerate sin in the dorms. Soon, I would accept the fact it was not the former staff's idea to quit; God simply allowed the spirit of discord to run its course. It ultimately led to a cleansing. Painful, no doubt about it . . . but necessary.

The underground dissention had been revealed and then dismissed. That spirit was not incorporated in this class—God had greater things in mind. God will work all things together for our good, if we let Him.

God's Timing

God brings special people into our lives to build us up—especially during times we feel alone and forsaken. That's when I found this song written just for me sometime earlier by Jeff Cogswell, a special friend. I was overwhelmed when this great man of God and extraordinary musician asked me to meet him in the small chapel of the Teen Challenge ministry in Rural Ridge, Pennsylvania, where I was then directing the women's program. Richard Turgeon was the executive director.

"I was up late last night writing a song about you," Jeff said.

"You're kidding!" I responded. "About me?"

"Yes, about you! Want to hear it?"

"Are you joking? Of course I want to hear it!"

"Then meet me in the chapel," he said, turning to leave the room. Jeff was born blind, but he knew the building like the back of his hand. I scurried to put the mail I had in my hands in the proper mailboxes, and then rushed to the chapel.

Sitting at the piano, Jeff played a wonderful tune I had never heard before.

"That's beautiful! It makes me want to clap my hands and hum along! Thank God, it is not sad!" I said facetiously, letting Jeff know I was in the room as we both laughed. He always teased me because he knew I would always choose lively songs that caused the people to rejoice.

"It's just the tempo you like; just don't sing along," Jeff said, laughing because singing is certainly not my gift! "I've named the song 'Special People' because you are special to the clients here. Listen to the words."

Special People

I remember the day that You called me
and You said, "Follow Me
in a life of service, faith, and victory."

I remember how You took my old life
and brought it to a stop,
and You put a new one in its place
and You rearranged my heart.

CHORUS

Oh, You called me to be Yours
and I love You with all my soul.
Yes, You called me to serve special people,
and Your blood has made me whole.

I remember when I was so lonely
I thought that nobody cared,
but You reached down and truly loved me.
Now my heartbreak You have repaired.

You'll be with me in the hard times
as I travel down life's road.
You will send Your people along
to help me bear the load.

I remember the day You filled me
with Your power from up above
to empower the gift of service
and to bear the fruit of love.

From Chaos to Christ

For twenty years, I dealt with one addiction after another—prescription pills, laxatives, diuretics, and alcohol. My life was completely unmanageable, and my family was in chaos. I craved something—anything—to help me deal with the pain. So I began seeing a therapist who prescribed antidepressants and sedatives, and I began abusing those. Often, I retreated to my bed, being depressed and suicidal. In reality, I didn't want to die; I wanted to know how to live. I craved peace and normalcy, only I didn't even know what "normal" was.

My pastor told me about Peniel. Within two weeks, I was in Johnstown.

Peniel has shown me the way to live soberly, normally, and whole. Through my counselor, Carlene Larmond, I learned "I can do all things through Christ who strengthens me" (Phil. 4:13 NKJV). I thank God for her, for Dr. Spellman and her obedience to fulfill the vision God gave her for Peniel, and for Pastor Spellman and his teaching of foundational biblical principles.

Just as Jacob wrestled and met God face-to-face, I have truly wrestled and won my freedom.—*Frances (Georgia)*

CHAPTER 10

CHOOSE YOU THIS DAY

Christian television has always been important to me. During those early days when the Enemy was attacking Peniel, Christian programming was especially encouraging. Even today as I engage in office chores, I am able to concentrate and focus when certain sounds are in the background . . . like a television program.

I used to regularly watch *The Voice of Freedom* with Reverend Jim Nichols on WGCB, our local Christian station. The program exposed pending and present issues that threatened the foundation of the Christian faith.

The drug epidemic was one of the concerns, so I contacted him about allowing me to address it in a future broadcast. Reverend Nichols decided to first visit the facility to see the work for himself before making a commitment. I had no idea the impact this meeting would make on my life for the next several years.

We met for more than two hours. Finally, we brought the meeting to a close with an invitation for me to be a guest on his program. "Absolutely . . . and thank you!" I said. The date was confirmed.

Follow-up Broadcasts

The broadcast was great, and I found it exciting. I was surprised when Reverend Nichols invited me back to do three follow-up broadcasts. Wow! We were getting the word out about Peniel. People were learning that God had the only answer for the addiction epidemic sweeping our nation, and they could find the answer here at Peniel.

I would wear my best business suit. *I should dress, but not overdress*, I thought. What about my makeup? I would need to do it myself; I did not like the way they made me up for the first taping! The makeup was too light and the alternative they had at the studio was entirely too dark, so I would need to do my own makeup this time. This was exciting! God was opening a new door.

Dr. Nichols received such tremendous response from those broadcasts that he invited me to be his permanent cohost. *The Voice of Freedom* took on a new atmosphere. Dr. Nichols encouraged me privately to continue to engage in friendly banter with him on the air, while still discussing some of the most disturbing matters of the day.

The audience loved it. They enjoyed the fact that the broadcast was not a "soapbox" pushed by the station, but rather an exchange of ideas; and, most importantly, it was an exposition of current events. We invited some of the most interesting guests who eloquently articulated hidden movements that the church might be informed. My assignment was to make sure our audience easily understood the information presented by our guests. We would use the questions I asked to make any clarification I felt was needed.

Often, I met our guests for the first time on the set. I preferred it that way because I was hearing the presentation for the first time along with our audience; therefore, the questions and answers would be spontaneous.

This program took off! It was so popular that the station sponsored a weekly program in addition to our daily *Voice of Freedom* broadcast. We called the new program *Getting*

Together. The format of this program was to interview local ministries. I was so happy to be a part of inviting local pastors, musicians, and support ministries to come and share what God was doing. Of course, I was sure to invite my friends to be our guests. *What a blessing to be able to give for a change!*

Although I did not schedule the guests, I could submit names. I encouraged invitations to the smaller ministries that were doing a great work but did not have much publicity or finances. It was also thrilling to meet individuals who had overcome adversity to accomplish great things for God. This broadcast also took off from the beginning! In today's vernacular, it "went viral."

The Marion Spellman Show

Finally, the owner of the station called me in his office. "Marion, the station is going on satellite."

"Satellite?" I asked. "What does that mean to our coverage?"

"It means that our coverage has expanded . . . a lot!" he said, laughing. "I want to give you your own show."

"My own show? Are you serious?"

"Yes. I know you can do this!"

"But I don't think I will have time," I said. "I am already burning the midnight oil trying to keep up with the center, and my husband is in a master's degree program in an accelerated course at Lincoln University. I don't see how I can take on another broadcast."

"I have thought about that," he said. "Which broadcast do you want to give up to do *The Marion Spellman Show*? Think about it and get back to me in a couple of days."

I left his office in a fog. What was happening? Was God changing His assignment for me? Everything I had done in the media had prospered, and there was one problem after another at Peniel. I was afraid to even answer the phone for fear of another unsolvable problem at the center.

On the ride home, I told myself, *This is God! No more building searches; no more budgets; no more utility bills; no more staff problems; no more betrayals. Yes! This was definitely God!*

After all, I was turning down stacks of invitations to minister in churches of our guests and our audience.

I waited a couple of days before calling the owner of the studio; I wanted to be able to tell myself I had prayed about it because this was a big decision. Finally, I asked the owner's secretary if I could see him after our regularly scheduled taping. She said yes without asking him, as if she had been told in advance.

Meeting with the owner, I told him, "I decided to give up the *Getting Together* program and keep *Voice of Freedom,* and then start the new show."

"Good girl, we will give you time enough to pull your staff together for the new program. I would like it to be a Christian variety show."

"Yes, I could do that! I have just the person who has the energy and the passion to help me with the broadcast—Lisa McAfee! She is smart, extremely personable, and a follow-through person. She excels in the midst of reversals and problems. She is Spelly's secretary . . . but that's no problem," I chuckled.

The Marion Spellman Show

In a month or so, we aired *The Marion Spellman Show* with a live audience. They would ask the questions of our guests. Guess who our first audience was? You guessed it—our students! Soon, the community was writing in for free tickets to the tapings. Yes, it was God all right. The studio was only one hour away from the center; I was juggling my office duties, and all was well with the world.

Spelly and I would go into a store, and people would recognize me. "Marion Spellman, I watch you all the time," they would say.

Smiling, I would humbly say, "Thanks! I really appreciate it."

I had purposed I would not mismanage the extra attention, and I would never be rude or irritated at anyone. After all, I was working for God!

Big Changes

All was well until the move to Somerset. Now the studio was nearly six hours roundtrip. The residents had to get up before 5 o'clock, drive to the studio, sit all day as we taped six shows, and then drive back to the center. Besides this, I still had to come back to the studio for another full day each week to tape the *Voice of Freedom* broadcast. *But, yes,* I said, *God is in it!*

One day in my office, I met with one of our clients in treatment.

"Mrs. Spellman, I am so excited to meet with you. Thanks for taking the time for me." Something was wrong with what he was saying. What I was hearing him say in my spirit was, *You are never here, and you really do not have time for us.* I heard the Spirit of the Lord say, *Choose! Choose what I have called you to do . . . or choose* The Marion Spellman Show. *You cannot have them both.*

For weeks I had privately pondered what God was saying to me; now I knew.

"I choose what You have called me to do," I said, already missing the attention and the accolades. "Lord, if You are not with me, I cannot survive."

I had to acknowledge I liked the applause, and I enjoyed being recognized. It felt good knowing I had a part in the rising ratings at the studio, but I could finally say it was not the Lord's will for me.

I wish I could say I gave it all up and did not look back. However, I spent time in the presence of God praying I would not return to TV when facing hard places that would be inevitable in growing Peniel. At this writing, I do not regret the decision I made. In fact, I am more thankful today than ever before. I am not sure if I would not have fallen into the popular "prosperity gospel" doctrine . . . but God knows! What I am sure is God has not called me to *The Marion Spellman Show*. Instead, He has called me to His program.

From Addict to Stylist

On July 19, 1999, I came to Peniel. As a result of using crack cocaine on and off for thirteen years, I was depressed, angry, confused, and needed to get my life back on track. After realizing I could not do this on my own, I made up my mind to do whatever it took to get my life back together.

After completing the program, I worked as a hair stylist for six years. Then, in October 2006, I opened Cassandra's Hair Studio. I have been married for eight years and have four daughters. I have been a homeowner for twelve years. I am grateful to Peniel and the entire staff for their dedication and faithfulness to the program and to God.—*Cassandra (Pennsylvania)*

CHAPTER 11

BY HIS STRIPES

No one wants to hear the word *cancer*. It stops you in your tracks and causes your heart to skip a beat. It brings mortality front and center. Sounds are imperceptible and your vision is blurred.

I was not a preventative-care person. I did not have regular checkups or the recommended annual physicals. I thought I was too busy! Did I say *too busy*? Now I'm a believer.

An Interruption in the Ministry

It was on an ordinary day with no fanfare, pomp, or circumstance that I thought I felt something. *Was this a lump? Hmm!* I thought, *No concern!* After all, it was not painful; it was not sore or even noticeable. But it became more of a concern when Spelly touched me and promptly asked, "Babe, what is that? You better have this checked out."

Over time, I became more aware but still not overly alarmed. The next Sunday at church, I asked my sister, Lori, to come in my office. I said, "Hey Lo, feel this. Do you feel anything unusual?"

She ran her hand over the area in my body and felt the protrusion. Immediately, she went in prayer, resolutely running her anointed hands over the area that was under attack. She firmly proclaimed this was not from God and we were not going to accept this invader. She refused to see this as anything other than an interruption in the ministry.

After church, I casually mentioned this new event to Trisha Eagleson, a capable nurse practitioner who was a blessing to our family during Momma's illness. Trisha is a proven sister in the Lord to me, and a founding and faithful member of the Peniel Praise Community Church. I guess I already knew what she would say. Even though she is qualified to write prescriptions, I have never known her to diagnose anyone in a casual conversation. Her response was always the same: "Let's see what the doctor has to say."

I could tell by the tone of her voice that she was very concerned. "Sissy, listen to me!" she said sternly. "You need to make an appointment with the doctor." Knowing my procrastination history, she continued, "Do you want me to make the appointment for you?"

"No, I'll make it," I promised.

"OK. I recommend Dr. Gerald Gargiola. He is the best! I will call you tomorrow with his number."

Now I was numb with fear. I had cared for my mother and my dad during their illnesses. Having seen what sickness could do in a body, I feared what would happen to me. I interact with clients and their families who live in a world of denial every day; now it was my turn to deal with hard, cold truth.

Facing Reality

I was forced to admit that I often question why people make excuses, blame others, and refuse to see the truth of the results they are reaping from their life choices. Certainly, it was as clear as the nose on their faces! *What was it going to take?* I would sarcastically say to myself. But this was different—this was about me! The possibilities were too awful and frightening for me to face.

Trisha called the next Tuesday. “Sissy, did you make the appointment?” There was a brief silence.

“Not yet,” I said softly, “but I will.”

“No,” she said, nearly interrupting. “I’ll make it for you.”

“I promise—I will make it right now!” I said.

Sensing my fear, she said, “I’ll go with you, if you’d like.”

“No, Spelly would never allow me to go without him—you know that!” I said as we both laughed.

“You’ve got that right,” she said. “But I don’t want to have to involve him in this, so you had better call today!”

Immediately I made an appointment with Dr. Gargiola, who specializes in breast cancer. He was personable and appeared to be very thorough, but definitely all business. Just as I suspected, after an embarrassing examination, he promptly ordered a biopsy.

Sleepless nights followed—I was tossing and turning, not knowing what the outcome of the biopsy would be. I believed my faith in God was intact, but why was I so fearful?

Susan Henry—A Great Woman of Faith

I work with a wonderful woman of God who has been diagnosed with cancer three times in the same area of her body. Susan Henry has served as my trusted friend and secretary for eighteen years. She is one of the greatest women of faith I have ever known.

Susan E. Henry, Secretary

When I told her what the doctor had said, she did not hesitate to retell the glorious account of what God had done for her. In every appropriate juncture, she would assure me of what He would also do for me. She meticulously rehearsed that, in spite of what the doctors had predicted, she has remained cancer-free for over thirty-six years.

Still, the same question haunted me and even tormented me. *Why was I so fearful? Why wasn't my strong faith in God kicking in*? After all, I had prayed with countless women in similar situations. Three Sundays before this discovery, God had given me a word for the congregation. God had used me to say to a full house that someone in the congregation was being healed of breast cancer. Three women I did not know came to the altar, declaring God was speaking to them.

I had preached deliverance. The anointing given to Peniel was one of restoration and healing broken lives. We were positioning men and women to receive divine intervention by Almighty God on a daily basis. Peniel staff members are all familiar with our spiritual position in the treatment arena: God first; then, professional treatment techniques. Countless times I have said to a counselor, "The secular community is able to identify and even provide names and categories for humanity's problems, but the ultimate solution is exclusively in the hands of God. God has anointed Peniel to speak life into dead situations."

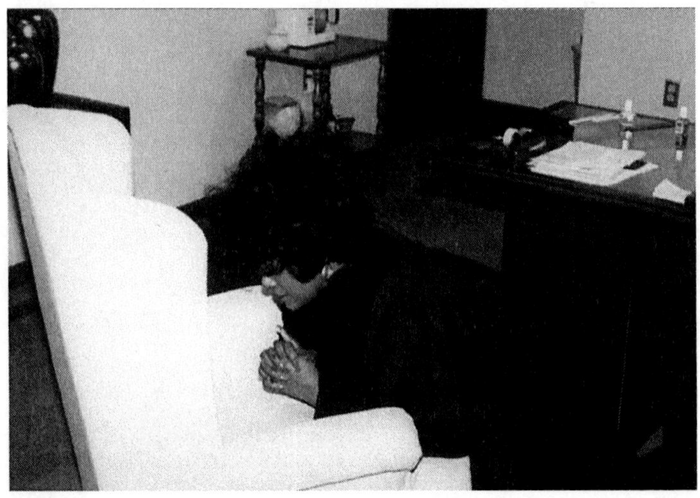

Interceding for Personal Healing

Now I was face-to-face with my own mortality. As I lay awake in bed, I had horrifying flashes and found myself repeating, "I'm so afraid, Lord. I still have ministry in me, God, and I still have work to do for You." I knew cancer was a formidable enemy. In fact, this was the greatest enemy I had ever encountered.

I will never forget the sudden attack of fear that took place in my home. Suddenly I had trouble breathing, and for a moment, I could not even see. The spirit of terror had gripped me so intensely that I experienced hysterical blindness—a temporary condition resulting from great trauma. I was reacting to the devastating circumstances I was only imagining.

The Diagnosis

The biopsy was back! As Job once said, "The thing which I greatly feared is come upon me" (3:25). Spelly sat silently as Dr. Gargiola gave us the news. I can repeat his words verbatim: "Well, the biopsy came back—and it was malignant." He was silent for a moment, as if he was waiting for us to digest the report. He continued, "It is treatable and it is curable, but you are definitely not going to have any fun. Treatment will be difficult! You will lose your hair and you will be very sick."

I heard nothing but the devastating words: "The mass is malignant." I looked at my husband. Without a word, I knew he understood me—I was asking him to make this all go away! Spelly, looking directly at the doctor, sat silently without any expression.

Finally, he looked at me. Again, without a word, he confidently spoke to me: *It's all right, Babe! Everything is going to be all right.*

The bizarre twenty-minute ride home was a blur. I felt I had been transported to *The Twilight Zone*.

The Fight of My Life

When I finally could talk about it, I kept asking Spelly, "What did the doctor say?" He would never verbally acknowledge the malignant mass; rather, he would begin with the doctor saying, "It is treatable and it is curable." Spelly went into fighting mode. We spoke to the Lord, and He gave Spelly the plan.

First, we would earnestly seek the Lord, asking Him to heal me, but we would only ask once. We would thank Him for the answer. We were clear this was not a formula, and it was not a trick to move God. No! This was about us and our faith. We accepted the fact that we did not need a crisis to encourage God to move. He had never stopped moving in our lives.

Next, we would celebrate Communion together every morning. We would boldly and specifically affirm the powerful truth that Christ's stripes are still God's antidote for disease, and they were able to heal me.

Finally, we would operate in the liberty given to the saints. We still belonged to Him, and it was important that the spiritual babies in our ministry saw it through our lives, not only by what we said.

The closer I got to God, the more the fear gradually subsided. Notwithstanding, the cold facts remained: I was facing the fight of my life. This aggressive attack was capable of taking my life.

In my struggle to organize Peniel, I had watched God as He supernaturally grew the ministry. I had witnessed financial miracle after miracle and had even overcome the crushing heartbreak of betrayal. Now my concern was whether I was able to activate the same anointing that has sustained me all of these years. One thing was settled in my heart: I would do the work of Almighty God all the days of my life. This attack would not be enough for me to abandon my post.

Clinging to God's Word

God had victoriously taken me through countless trials, setbacks, and heartaches over the years: losing my brother, Puddin . . . ministering to my ailing father with round-the-clock care . . . later doing the same for my beloved mother . . . and even later losing Spelly's brother, who was brutally murdered. God was there with us through it all. I told myself, *God yet lives, and I too will live.*

We prepared for the uncertainty of extensive chemotherapy. I could cling to the wonderful Word of God and the glorious faithfulness of my marvelous Savior. He had never left me in the past, and He would be with me now.

Spiritual Warfare

My family, church, and staff rallied around us and prayed. Dr. Peggy Scarborough, a co-pastor in South Carolina, and a longtime and faithful friend, stood with me. Spelly and I were with her when she went through the same challenge more than twenty years prior to my experience. Peggy called me twice a week to speak directly against the cancer. She would demand my body to obey the Word and the will of God. She would remind me I was to be in good health and prosper. Anything other than that was unacceptable. I had prayed the same prayer for her those many years ago, and she is alive and changing lives on a daily basis. She has founded a school of healing. She teaches men and women weekly to position themselves so God will touch them.

Then there was Lori's husband—my brother-in-law, André. You have to know Elder André Curry. *Every day* he called to pray with me. Now when André prays, bring a lunch, because he is going to take his time to rehearse God's attributes, describe God's power, and then talk about how God knows how to care for what belongs to Him. Unless he thinks of something else about our great God, he will place his petition before Him. When André called, I would pick up the phone with a hello. The next thing I would hear was, "Hey, Sissy! Ready to pray?" and the spiritual war was on!

During the next four or five months, I was unable to get much sleep. Satan would attack my faith in God unmercifully at night. One morning about 3:30 a.m., I got up and began to read my Bible, but it was not registering. Finally, determined that I would not stay awake another night, I cried out, "God, help me! Please help me!" God led me to call Dr. Barbara Amos, who has been a dear friend for many years. She is the founding pastor of the Faith Deliverance Church in Norfolk, Virginia. *OK*, I thought. *I'll call her in the morning.* No, I could almost hear the Lord say, "Call her now."

Slowly, I dialed her number; immediately, she answered. Tears rolling down my cheeks, I simply said, "I am not doing well . . . I can't sleep . . . I am not going to make it!" Even though I had awakened her from a deep sleep, she instinctively knew I did not need a sermon. Also, I did not need her to take a personal survey to access my faith in God. I already knew if we live godly, we are going to suffer. Although I didn't know what I needed to hear, she did! She gently and softly began to pray, acknowledging the weakness of humanity and the strength of God. She focused on my situation but not specifically on me.

She acknowledged we were under attack and in great need for His intervention. She confirmed our love for God and that we were in an hour of need. She used words like *we, our*, and *us*. Was she confused? Was she still awake? No, she was deliberately praying as if it was she who was calling me for prayer. She had intentionally entered into this arena with me.

This was no longer just my issue—she was taking it on as well. Soon, I was no longer hearing Dr. Amos, but I was able to hear Christ. What an experience! After that night, I did not have to deal with this same demon of fear.

In the coming months, letters, cards, and phone calls poured in, and the faith of those who understood my battle stood with me. It would be two years before I would know the outcome. Working through the pain and the fear, I stayed immersed in the Word and work of God. My beloved husband provided unwavering support, holding fast to the position that God can heal, God will heal, and God had healed me. It did not matter who had died from this or what their individual story was, God was with us! As the Scripture says, "I would live and not die, and I would declare the work of the Lord" (see Ps. 118:17).

Today I am doing great, and I give all the glory to our awesome God!

Delivered From Depression

After several attempts to control my thirty-two-year abuse of antidepressants and heroin, I had given up. I had no hope left. Year after year, my pastor told me I needed long-term treatment.

My children did not even want to be around me. They were afraid they would find me dead. One of my children moved out on his own. My fifteen-year-old moved to his sister's house. My fourteen-year-old went to his grandmother's home every chance he got, and my eleven-year-old went to my friends.

Finally on November 2, 1999, I came to Peniel, and my life was restored. Now I am living sober, and I have goals for my family and myself. I have learned not to compromise. Through the classes, individual counseling, and observing godly women around me, I learned to be a woman of Christian character.

My relationships with my family, my church, and the Lord Jesus have been restored. I give God all the honor and glory for the good work He is doing in my life. He who began a good work in me is faithful to complete it (Phil. 1:6).—*Deborah (Pennsylvania)*

CHAPTER 12

WHY PENIEL WORKS

Catching the Vision
(Reflections From Becki Guyer)

My name is Becki Guyer. For many years, my name and Peniel were almost synonymous because it was as much a part of me as my next breath.

Becki Guyer

I met Dr. Marion Spellman while serving as a home missionary/counselor at Teen Challenge in Rural Ridge, Pennsylvania. She was the director of the female program there, and the first time I heard her minister, I knew I wanted to be mentored by this amazing woman of God.

A year later, Dr. Spellman relocated her family to Camp Hill, where she had been offered a position with Pennsylvania's commissioner of Corrections. I returned to my hometown of Johnstown and remained in touch.

Through her position within the penal system, Dr. Spellman became aware of the desperate need for a Christian-oriented rehabilitation program due to the horrendous statistics of drug-related crime. The Lord began to speak to her regarding His vision, and Peniel was born.

The Dream

I wanted to be a part of this work—I wanted to help make it happen! It began as a dream on paper, dictated at Dr. Spellman's kitchen table during marathons that would last through the night! I would be delirious, barely able to hold my head up, but Dr. Spellman had fire in her bones and was on a roll! She would splash me with cold water, or whatever she had to do to kick me back into gear. Since this was way before the computer age, we worked strictly with pen and paper. My hand was in a permanent cramp.

Birthing the Ministry

For several months, I maintained my job back in Johnstown and drove to Harrisburg on my days off to fulfill my duties at Peniel. Then I relocated there, and acquired a small apartment three minutes away from our facility, which was owned by Christians.

We had no income. God was our source. We prayed in every dollar and we were thankful for every blessing, no matter how small, and God never failed to meet our needs. My church supported me as a home missionary, and various individuals "adopted" me as their personal missionary, pledging monthly support. My bills were always paid, and I always had a roof over my head and food on my table. The Lord fed me from His hand!

From the beginning, I knew I was called to be Dr. Spellman's secretary. The problem was that I did not type! I had never had clerical training. I trusted God to give me a "crash course" and depended on Him to make me worthy. During that time, I kept a journal. Reading it now is almost comical; I was as green as they come.

We were a new ministry with an unfamiliar name. We had to find our place within the Christian community and meet government guidelines to obtain licensing as a drug-and-alcohol rehabilitation program. This was no easy task as we had so little with which to work.

We never knew what the Lord had in store for us on any given day. It was an incredible period of spiritual growth and development. Being young both chronologically and as a Christian, I had a childlike faith. There was so little that could be logistically planned; it was all by faith. We followed God's instructions as He revealed them to Dr. Spellman, even when we didn't understand the rationale. My expectations then were only that the Lord would honor His Word and guide our steps.

The Visionary

As founder and president, Dr. Spellman was the visionary, and I can imagine that what God revealed to her was overwhelming. I, on the other hand, could only hold onto the promise of the vision. I could not see further than the moment at hand; it was too much! Even when we acquired our current facility back in 1993, it was a former construction company with a dilapidated trucking dock in the back that was going to eventually be renovated and become our dormitories.

Dr. Spellman saw what it would become, while I could not see past the mess before my eyes. Although I tried, I could only hold onto the vision and trust God to accomplish it. The Lord raised up professional architects and engineers who believed in our work and gave their time and talents to help us. Days, weeks, and months of meetings, drawings, and plans . . . and finally the finished product emerged! When I reflect on where we started—the log cabins with no insulation—I am mesmerized with all God has done at Peniel.

Worth Every Hardship

What we would perceive as hardships today were more like adventures then. In each situation, we knew the Lord was going to work . . . we just never knew the *how*.

When Reverend Spellman came on the scene, he added another dimension and helped to complete the "recipe," as he had the gift of faith. When the bills began pouring in and the income was far from what we needed, he believed that somehow, some way—with no doubt, no loss of sleep, no fretting—God was going to come through in His own time, and He *always* did!

Having little income, I had no way to buy a car, but the Lord provided. An owner of a car dealership, Al Bitner, became a friend of Peniel, and he gave the ministry several vehicles, including three vans. He told the Spellmans that God had told him to help us. My favorite was a Volkswagen Beetle. It had no heat, and I sometimes scraped ice off the inside windshield as I went! Yet, nothing plowed through the snow like that little "bug"!

Big Heartbreak

The biggest hardship and heartache of working in such a ministry was losing some of the people who had become family to me. Prior lifestyles of abuse and health neglect sometimes took its toll, and we suffered the devastating loss and grief of death at times with some of our own. However, how glorious that we were able to celebrate their homegoings, since through Peniel, each had a "face-to-face experience" with the Lord Jesus Christ!

Nothing quite breaks your heart as when those whom the Lord has chosen, those handpicked to enter through the doors of Peniel, are set free from the devastating web of addiction only to go back to "Egypt." The successes are many. The testimonies are amazing, and those who are longtime alumni are precious fruit of the work, but those few whom the devil fooled tore our heart to shreds.

A Face-to-Face Encounter

The name *Peniel* is taken from Genesis 32:30, where Jacob wrestled with an angel all night long. When God finally blessed him, he said he would name the place of his struggle *Peniel*, "for I have seen God face to face, and my life is preserved." We built this treatment program on that foundational declaration. Although our rehabilitation and therapy model is intense, it is face-to-face encounters with Jesus Christ that changes lives. That's where the transformation journey really begins. The Peniel experience is unique for each person. The resident's individualized treatment plan reaches beyond personal addiction issues to include the family or significant others to collaborate and support.

The staff at Peniel is phenomenal! Professionalism and Christian character are nonnegotiable personnel standards. Patience, hope, and love are prerequisites for bonding together as a team. The staff has a strong commitment to help every client reach their potential.

I will always remain a part of Peniel. The Spellmans and staff will forever be in my heart. Amazing changes have taken place in the last thirty years as far as the physical structure that houses Peniel. There are new faces, new processes, and new challenges, but one thing will forever remain the same—the Peniel experience!

As a drug-and-alcohol rehabilitation program, Peniel deals with the whole person—body, soul, and spirit. Many rehabilitation programs work with the body and soul through therapy and counseling. The difference with Peniel is we introduce each student to their spirit and show them how to give it to God. From there, therapy is intense as the clients look within themselves, seeing things that are often very painful to see and realize. Only then can they begin to grow, leaving the old things behind and pressing forward with new hope and promise. Of course, Satan is busy and the battles are constant. The staff and counselors fight for their clients and intercede for them in prayer.

I believe it works because, from day one, those coming to Peniel for help are pointed directly to God as the source of their help. As they get to personally know Him, they are able to draw strength from Him, knowing within their hearts that He loves them and hears their cries.

A Godly Mentor

Through the past thirty-five years, I have tried to express what Dr. Spellman means to me, and I have concluded there just are no words. Back in 1977 when I first met Dr. Spellman at Teen Challenge, I wanted to serve under her and glean from her everything I possibly could. She saw something in me and answered that call.

Dr. Spellman is my "mother" in the Lord. She raised me from the ground up spiritually. Although I had already been saved and was churched when I met her, I was not discipled. I knew nothing about accountability and the many little things that matter so much when trying to accomplish big things. Dr. Spellman taught me, mentored me, and grew me. She was hard on me—hard to the point that I wanted to give up many times! But deep in my heart, I knew she was right, and I wanted more than anything to be all God wanted me to be. So I would bite the bullet and endure!

As Dr. Spellman's secretary, she poured herself into me as we were together nearly 24/7 during those beginning years of building the program. I would travel with her, and that time was utilized for teaching and learning.

Aside from being her secretary, Dr. Spellman was my best friend. Her family became my family. My favorite times were when her mom and her Aunt Sis would come to visit, and we would tell stories of Dr. Spellman's childhood. We would laugh till we cried!

Serving in that position probably allowed me to see beyond what so many fail to see in terms of what Dr. Spellman's calling and responsibilities are. It is demanding for all of the staff, for ministry is far from just a nine-to-five job. But Dr.

Spellman—the leader, CEO, executive director, head honcho, or whatever title you want to give her—is responsible for every facet, every decision, every dime that is raised and spent. She is the one whom authorities will come to for any problem, whom bill collectors will come to for money, whom family members will come to for answers, whom staff members will come to for decisions, and whom students will come to for help.

In addition to all this, she has a personal life and family members with their own needs. She has this monumental weight she has been asked to carry, and she does so with such dignity and grace that you know the Lord walks beside her and dwells within her. Yet, she is a human being with emotions and feelings like any woman. I think of the song written by Dolly Parton that says, "She's a sparrow when she's broken, but she's an eagle when she flies." That is Marion Spellman.

Recently while working at my part-time job at a local supermarket, a guy came through my line and we were laughing and joking about a couple of his purchases. Suddenly, he said, "I know you from somewhere! You are so familiar! I know that I know you!"

"Really?" I said. "You wouldn't happen to have gone to Peniel at any time, would you?"

He nearly fell over as he reached across the belt to give me a big bear hug! He was in Peniel more than twenty years ago! He is doing excellent, and is pastoring a church on the north side of Pittsburgh! He expressed his thanks to God for Peniel and Dr. Spellman's vision. There he stood—a trophy of her obedience to God's call on her life! Every person this young man reaches in his ministry is a fruit of Dr. Spellman's labors as well!

The love I have for Dr. Spellman cannot be put into words. Her wisdom never fails to astound me, and I dearly miss the closeness and opportunities of gleaning from her as I did when I worked with her at Peniel. All she poured into me is being manifested in my life every day . . . I am a part of her fruit. One cannot imagine the crowns that await her in heaven.

My Family

Often I wonder where I would be, and what I would be, had I not met Dr. Spellman and become a part of Peniel. Every choice I make, as well as my perspective on things, is influenced by what I learned there.

Now I work for a large health-insurance company. The work environment was a huge culture shock when I first left Peniel. Because of all I learned and experienced there, fulfilling the requirements now asked of me is a piece of cake! So many people whine and complain about the smallest things—it boggles my mind. I believe it is because of this that I was the first in my department chosen to be a telecommuter. For the past five years, I have enjoyed working my job from home. No commuting, no makeup. Hey, I can stay in my pajamas if I want! Such trust would have never been given to me had I not learned what I did at Peniel.

Even though now I reside in Pittsburgh, about an hour and a half away from Johnstown, I still attend Peniel Praise Community Church. And I still feel elated at every graduation ceremony. The Spellmans and the staff at Peniel are my family.

Passing the Torch (Reflections From Marion Spellman)

When Becki realized she would indeed be relocating to Pittsburgh, it was gratifying to know she had a hand in mentoring the person who would become my secretary. Becki had patiently taken the time to train Susan Henry to fulfill her vacancy. Susan was more capable and professional than we had realized. She had developed virtues and skills that would complement my office, and God was waiting to use them. She had no way of knowing He had been preparing her all the time.

But why would we be surprised that Susan was so equipped and up to the task? God had already designed the perfect plan for every season of Peniel, and this was previously part of His master plan.

Susan is one of the kindest and most caring people I had ever known. She has never been in search for a position of elevation but a place of service. She has been tremendously instrumental in helping us to attain and maintain perfect state inspection scores year after year. She and her husband, Bill, are committed to the work of God, and they have given their lives to His cause.

The Open Door (Reflections From Susan Elizabeth Henry)

In January 1996, the start of a new year full of promise, we at Peniel found ourselves praying fervently for a new secretary for Dr. Spellman. Becki was gone; she had moved to Pittsburgh. As Dr. Spellman's personal secretary from the early days of Peniel, she had been an integral part of the ministry.

Who could ever take Becki's place? I wondered. Becki personified excellence and professionalism in everything she did. She had become a mentor to me and also a dear friend. I had no idea then what God was preparing for me.

Four years earlier, I had come to Peniel from my church in Canada, which was located in a drug-infested part of Toronto. After failed attempts to help restore some individuals who were addicted to drugs, our church realized people needed more than what we could offer them in our worship services. It became clear that long-term treatment was the answer.

After an intense search, our dedicated pastor, Mary Jane Bilenduke, discovered Peniel. Every time she spoke to the congregation about this program, my heart was flooded with an unexplainable joy. Together with some of the congregation, she led us from Toronto to Somerset, Pennsylvania, to experience the 1991 graduation celebration. Since that time, let me emphatically say, "My life has never been the same!"

Recalling the disenfranchised people I had seen daily on the streets of Toronto, I was in awe as I witnessed the lives of these Peniel graduates. Also, I saw something in their lives that I felt was missing in my own. I can still hear myself praying, "Whatever it is, God . . . I want it!"

Seven months later, in March 1992, with a one-year sponsorship from my church of $75 per month, I traveled again to Somerset . . . but this time to join the staff of Peniel. With a mind-set to learn and serve wherever needed, I soon began working as the receptionist, and I loved it.

Upon arrival at work one morning, and after greeting Dr. Spellman, she looked straight at me and said, "If you will give me three years, you will hardly recognize yourself . . . and by the way, your 'husband' is here." I responded with a resounding, "Yes!" And her words actually came to pass!

In March 1995, while participating in our weekly staff devotions, suddenly I recalled the words Dr. Spellman had spoken. Yes indeed, it had been three years to the month, and just as she had said, wonderful things had taken place in my life. Right here at Peniel, I had met and married Bill Henry, the man of my dreams. Bill is one of Peniel's senior counselors and an elder in the Peniel Praise Community Church. We were married in the Spellmans' home on December 9, 1994.

Bill and I continually encourage each other to excel in life and in our service here at Peniel. Words cannot express the joy, comfort, and privilege it is for me to "go to war" each day with this veteran soldier. Bill was a member of the U.S. Secret Service uniform branch assigned to protect the president of the United States, and he has also served in the U.S. Marines. More importantly, he is a dedicated soldier of the Lord Jesus Christ and a proud graduate of Peniel.

Also by this time, under Dr. Spellman's incredible leadership, I had developed spiritually, having arrived at an entirely new place in my love relationship with the Lord and His Word, which had been my heart's longing and desire. And I had grown to become more effective in Christian ministry.

Then, just nine months later, Dr. Spellman said to the staff, "God is always getting someone ready to come up to bat." She was asking me to become her secretary! I thought for a moment and cautiously said, “Yes, I will accept this position,” though I was overwhelmed at what seemed to be a daunting challenge . . . and then I cried.

There were times when the center was under attack that Dr. Spellman would say, “The task is impossible; therefore, let us proceed.” As the days, weeks, and months passed, those words became a reality in my life as I learned to embrace my new assignment.

With Dr. Spellman’s steady leadership and patient support, together we began our exciting journey that has been nothing less than remarkable. To have a small part in repeatedly witnessing what God will do in transforming a broken life yielded to Him is one of the greatest of all blessings. We have continually seen the ministry grow and God making “a way for us, out of no way!” Yes, along with the victories, we have faced heartbreaking reversals and challenging disappointments, but we have faced them together, thank God. We have encouraged one another in the faith, maintained our stride, and continued pressing forward!

As I write this testimony, it has been eighteen amazing years and counting. I still consider it an incredible privilege to serve in the ministry as Dr. Spellman’s personal secretary and her armor-bearer. Just recently I had one of those “aha” moments” when I had to stop and say, “Wow, God! . . . I can hardly believe I get to do this!” Like Becki, who has passed the torch to me, I have been able to invest in others who have joined the team. “Now, let us proceed!”

Conquering Cocaine

I was at my lowest point in life due to crack cocaine. Waking up in the mornings to get another hit became my focus. I had separated myself from my wife, my children, and all my family members. I sold everything I had. I knew if I kept getting high, eventually I was going to have to face greater consequences.

However, God had the final say in my life. I thank the Lord for giving me a clear mind one Sunday morning to call my mother and ask for help. She told me about Peniel, and since I have been here, God has really blessed my family and me. Peniel has taught me how to be a responsible father and husband, but, most of all, how to be a responsible man of God.—*Walter (Virginia)*

CHAPTER 13

WORKING WITH CHAMPIONS

It has been an awesome privilege for my husband and me to serve in this ministry with so many giants in the body of Christ. For instance, it has truly been an honor to work so closely with both Rebecca (Becki) Elizabeth Guyer and Susan Elizabeth Henry. We learned to work together as a team. While both women always had tremendous ideas of their own, if God was going another way, they were able to redirect their energies toward the ultimate goal.

It has been a joy writing this book with Susan Henry and Wanda Griffith. The many days and nights Susan and I spent together will be a wonderful memory. How could we ever forget those times when Susan would kindly say, "Dr. Spellman, would you like me to call Bill so he can start getting ready to come and pick me up . . . since it's so late?" That would be her not-so-subtle hint!

At times, I would type and she would help me think through a thought; at other times, she would type and I would dictate what I was thinking. Then we would email the chapter to Wanda, who was editing this book. Wanda would invariably tell me I had a hanging participle . . . or she had to change a word because I had overused it . . . or because, grammatically, a certain word should be switched. I can still hear Wanda's admonition: "At some point, Marion, we will have to move on. You can't continue to rewrite." She was trying to say as kindly as she could, "Don't send me another insert or change."

Susan and I would chuckle. Wanda was wonderful to work with, and I look forward to writing another book with her . . . but Wanda is totally silent regarding that last remark! All in all, this has been an amazing experience!

Well, let's get back to the reason you bought this book. . . .

From the beginning, I envisioned Peniel as a long-term residential treatment facility committed to maintaining a biblical and permanent solution to various addictions. These dedicated women have been vital to helping us accomplish this goal.

Statistics and research reveal that a high percentage of criminal and addictive behavior result from poorly utilized leisure time. We have found this to be true; therefore, when developing a treatment plan, "down time" is given priority attention. Treatment needs are revealed by observing the residents' choices during recreational activities and leisure time. The purpose of the close observation by staff is to inform the clients, as well as evaluate and reinforce their spiritual and emotional growth, thereby assisting them in making a smooth reentry into society.

A Tour of Peniel

Peniel has continued to evolve. We started with one counselor for the complete program. My husband was it! Now, praise God, we have an impressive Christian counseling complement of men and women who are committed to our clients. We have dramatically increased our treatment alternatives to include various aspects of the client needs.

For example, our academic program was expanded and monitored by Linda. Our goal was to provide educational opportunities that would "jump-start" and, in some cases, reengage the client in a classroom setting. These students are now able to earn transferable college credits. It is not uncommon to see Linda in the computer lab working with ten former addicts who are laboring feverishly to submit their online college assignments in time to meet their deadlines. Linda is one of the warmest and most capable women I have ever known. She is smart, kind, and a team player. Although very unassuming, she knows who she is and is always willing to stay within her own lane to accomplish the overall goal of the organization. I am honored to say that Linda now serves as my administrative assistant.

Computer Lab

In another section of the building, you will find a group of clients working on a creative-arts presentation. Our staff member, Tony, is teaching them that their gifts have been consecrated and are no longer dedicated to entertaining; now they are using drama as another means of worshiping and witnessing about the God they have just discovered. They are interpreting a Christian song in preparation for a Sunday worship service.

What you are now hearing is the Peniel choir rehearsing. That sound is coming from our sanctuary, where Dr. Henry McKenzie Davis, our accomplished minister of music and the assistant pastor of the Peniel Praise Community Church, is doing more than merely teaching musical scales and breathing techniques. He is skillfully directing the synergy of about twenty-five men and women, teaching them to blend as a group, combining their talents in music. It is a part of his unique style to forgo rehearsal altogether and pull out a portable podium and begin to teach the deep truths of worship that is acceptable to God. This choir is downright awesome!

Dr. Davis is a genius, and because he can make the sound of chalk scratching on a blackboard melodious, our goals for the choir are much different than most. You don't have to know how to sing to join because our goals are different. We are always in a teaching mode. That being the case, I was sure I qualified to be in the choir. For years, I have threatened to join . . . to no avail. Dr. Davis' answer to me is always the same: "Don't call us; we'll call you." I'm still waiting for the call!

Inspiration Hallway

Let's go down this long, bright, peach-colored foyer. Visitors have named this corridor "Inspirational Hallway" because the quotes on the walls are so encouraging. Here is our spiritual adviser's office—Bishop Ronnie Brock is ministering to a client. Bishop Brock is responsible for assisting new clients in gaining an understanding of the various components of a church worship service. Besides preaching, there is nothing he enjoys more than introducing a client to God for the first time. It is also Bishop Brock's responsibility to gently interview and assess clients to make sure they clearly understand the principles of water baptism and know when they are spiritually ready to be baptized. He also prepares them for receiving Communion.

Let's go to the kitchen where Kim, our culinary director, is in his glory. With him is a phase-four preceptor who is learning to make his famous fried chicken. No one makes it like Kim. Our goal is to teach our clients the basic fundamentals of cooking and how to prepare healthy meals. This department is also responsible for teaching basic table manners and proper dining etiquette. Kim joins the list of culinary staff who quickly became my husband's best friends!

I noticed you were looking in the pantry while we were near the kitchen. You are probably amazed at the quantity of supplies stored there. You just missed Dr. Barbara M. Amos, founder and pastor emeritus, and Pastor Sharon S. Riley, senior pastor of Faith Deliverance Christian Center, along with members of their team. They have driven an eighteen-wheel tractor-trailer truck all the way from Roanoke, Virginia, to Peniel. It took several hours and all of our guys, along with our male staff, to unload the supplies they brought. These supplies will last for months. How does one say "thank you" for that type of love and effort?

On the second floor you will find Steve, who is always busy. He is the director of our research and development department. Steve is excellent at discovering and investigating the latest treatment trends, as well as the newest and most popular street drugs. Steve regularly schedules seminars designed to further equip our staff. Our goal is to to stay on the cutting edge.

Beside Steve's office is Reverend Durean Coleman, our public-relations director. Among his various responsibilities, Durean observes and monitors our effectiveness with the public. He is the spokesperson who receives community concerns, and together we develop an appropriate response. He creates Peniel literature and newsletters, and monitors our website updates. A former atheist, Durean is a son of this ministry who was saved in a Sunday-morning service after hearing my husband's message. He continued to attend the services, eager to grow and develop spiritually. Durean eventually became a part of the Peniel staff. Now a credentialed minister in the Church of God, my husband and I are thrilled to say Durean has never looked back. He is an anointed pulpit preacher who is committed to the work of God. He is a team player personified.

Durean's mother, Vicki, was also a committed atheist but now is a Peniel alumnus. She is a skilled and compassionate nurse who worked as hard as anyone I have ever met in order to regain her license. Recovering her credentials is a miracle and is precious to her. She has dedicated her gifts and talents to the work of God. This is not surprising because, by nature, Vicki is a very grateful person. In addition to her own conversion, she has had her two sons accept the Lord at Peniel, and their lives have never been the same.

Vickie serves as our resident nurse who works with the most wonderful doctor in the world, Larry Beatty, M.D. He has maintained an amazing standard of care for his patients. He is in such demand that often he has had to discontinue accepting new patients. If you wondered what ever happened to doctors with bedside manners, we have located him and he comes to Peniel once a week.

Those students you see with brooms and dust mops, and those others who are carrying out the trash, are receiving treatment. Sue and Deborah are monitoring the women, and outside is Chris and Jason escorting the male clients to vocational therapy. Here the residents are taught positive work ethics, leadership skills, and how to be a team player. Since work is an important part of their lives, it is essential for our clients to learn to function as responsible, sober individuals in the workplace. They are taught to maintain a positive attitude in day-to-day living. Sweeping a floor can be a boring chore until the client understands the importance of doing everything as unto the Lord.

Larry, our vocational director, places emphasis on character as well as work skills. He teaches the clients to be responsible, take initiative, and properly respond to authority. They must demonstrate through their behavior and outlook that they know how to cooperate within a designed structure. Spelly's acronym for *work* is "Worshiping Our Righteous King."

When Larry is not giving directions as the vocational director, you will probably find him in the gym. Larry loves "down time" with the guys. The gym and the connecting workout room are two of the greatest blessings of Peniel. The students certainly rejoice because of it. This full-sized professional gym was the result of Bishop Donnie and Barbara Smith leading the effort to provide for our students with a place to release their tensions and stress. Physical exercise not only benefits the body, but it also contributes to mental, emotional, and spiritual well-being.

Next to the gym is the John Nichols Workout Room. It is something to behold! The late Dr. Nichols made sure the best equipment was placed here. Dr. Gene Rice, who was the chairman of our board of directors at that time, officiated the dedication ceremony in Dr. Nichols' presence.

Do you have time to stop by the Jim and MaryLee Osipov Learning Center? Jim is an accomplished engineer in Johnstown, having supervised the construction of several prominent buildings. He is also a retired professor, having served at the University of Pittsburgh at Johnstown for many years. The Osipovs have invested countless hours to assist with the

The Osipov Learning Center

vast and costly renovation of this facility. Not only did Jim and MaryLee design the blueprints, but Jim also served as our project supervisor. If they would have charged Peniel for their services, the estimated cost would have been over $250,000. What they have done was clearly unto the Lord, and we shall forever be grateful to them.

Now let's go into the Peniel library. This is a vital component of the academic division of our program. It was designed by the late Dr. Ray H. Hughes, who was a personal friend of the Spellmans. Linda, his wife, is a fantastic woman in her own right. She serves on our board of directors as I write this book.

Would you like to visit our classrooms? We have four classes in session right now. Bishop T. D. Jakes—pastor of The Potter's House in Dallas (Texas), an international evangelist, and a well-known author—generously donated the funds for this project. This is but one of the many ways Bishop Jakes has been a blessing to this ministry. He has been the guest speaker for two Peniel graduations. Lives were changed and families were reunited during those services. Bishop Jakes has graciously made several video promos on behalf of Peniel. Both he and his lovely wife, Serita, have a burning passion for the lost and for individuals who are addicted to life-controlling substances.

Classroom

Let's stop by Cricket's "Drug Awareness" class. She is the supervisor of the female dorm and an awesome counselor and teacher. No one leaves her class the same. It does not matter how long it takes, Cricket is willing to wait and to labor with her clients. She will hang in there with the residents until they qualify or quit.

There's Bill, another one of our counselor/teachers, conducting his "Sexual Integrity" class. Bill encourages the guys to be brutally honest about their addictions to sex, gambling, pornography, the Internet, and overall promiscuity. I am not sure of the topic for this month, but the discussions are always candid. Bill is known for getting to the raw root of the problem.

Emily's classroom is next. She is also a credentialed counselor dealing with sensitive issues with our ladies. She teaches "Healing of Damaged Emotions."

I'm sorry we are unable to include our counseling wing during our tour. Confidential sessions are in progress. Dawn, who serves as our clinical supervisor, is highly skilled. In the other office is Shane, another one of our excellent counselors. He is conducting a family session. Shane has a wonderful demeanor that puts both clients and their families at ease during often painful sessions.

The closed door we have just passed is our boardroom. This is where the supervisors and primary counselors meet each week to review the progress of every client in our care.

Now we are at Jeff's office. Jeff is our fiscal manager. You might want to speak with him because he will be able to process the check you are about to give. Your gift will be gratefully invested in a student's life.

Most of the donations given are designated for specific projects. We are deeply grateful, because that is how we built this center. Still, we are in urgent need of consistent operating funds that will allow us to raise our staff's salaries as they certainly deserve. Maybe you are the answer to this prayer. Maybe God is speaking to your heart to write that large check to be applied to the staff-salary fund. It would be a great investment with eternal benefits, translating into rescuing lives!

Those were not merely blank faces you saw on our mini-tour of the facility; these are your sons and your daughters. They are your grandchildren, and your nieces and nephews. Or perhaps you have someone else in need of treatment. You are in the right place and this is the right time!

Since that is the case, we need to double back to Sarah's office. Sarah is the director of admissions. She is gentle, patient, and kind. She knows that department like the back of her hand. Sarah, together with the intake staff, will tirelessly work your referral through the induction process. This department—made up of Sarah, Stephen, and Cathy—has a genuine commitment to get the applicant help as soon as possible. They will do everything possible to find an empty bed.

Now you will want to set up a student account for your referral. Mary Jean will track every penny. She is known for keeping accurate financial records of each client's income and spending patterns. She is responsible for sending monthly reports to the primary counselors. Tracking client's spending habits provide tremendous insight regarding client choices. Money has the potential to interrupt the client's progress. We strive to teach the client to respect the power of money.

The staff's commitment to excellence is not only evident in the way clients are treated, but in the high ratings the facility and staff consistently receive by outside agencies who evaluate programs such as ours. Reversing the curse of addiction and dealing with an individual's personal issues are not easy tasks. But the staff pour their lives into the clients to teach them new responses to tempting situations and to challenge and change destructive thought patterns.

Outpatient Program

The Pennsylvania Department of Health Office of Drug and Alcohol Programs licenses Peniel as an outpatient facility. This component provides one-on-one and family counseling to individuals who are not in need of inpatient treatment, but who require intense professional care through prescheduled weekly appointments. Many outside agencies use this service.

The President's Council

I am forever grateful to the men and women who serve on this board. This is not an official group, and we do not have formal meetings. Their task is designed specifically to pray and to encourage me during difficult times, or when facing discouragement or challenges. The people on this board have made themselves available to help carry the load.

The Peniel Advisory Board

The organizing of the Peniel Advisory Board was sanctioned and approved by our board of directors. It is comprised of seven to nine community leaders. They have committed to assist Peniel in maintaining a positive image in the local community. These members introduce Peniel to educational facilities serving high-risk kids, churches, and other organizations that may benefit from the services we provide. Our goal is to be a blessing to those in need of our expertise.

The Advisory Board does not make policies, but they support our structure that has been established and approved by the Pennsylvania Department of Health, Office of Drugs and Alcohol Programs, and has been sanctioned by the Peniel Board of Directors.

Peniel Board of Directors and the Pennsylvania Administrative Bishop

On behalf of our board of directors and our present chairman, Dr. Michael Baker, and on behalf of Dr. Kenneth Bell, our pastor and our administrative bishop, we thank you for purchasing this book and for allowing us to share the Peniel story.

One Ingredient

Through Peniel, God is reaching His hand into prisons and detention centers. The success of Peniel is manifested everywhere through our graduates. We are on the streets of our cities and in our small towns telling the story of deliverance.

Here is the raw and frightening truth: Destructive, life-controlling addictions are here to stay. Families—good families—are destined for attack! This diabolical "cancer" named *addiction* has found its way into our comfortable homes and, in some cases, is even seated on the pews of our churches. The names of the drugs and the types of addictions will change, but the end result will remain the same. Death is the ultimate end for those who do not have the answer. Their future is as dark as history has ever recorded.

But here is the good news! The ongoing work of Peniel is a living testimony of God's magnificent ability to transform lives and to defeat every foe. If there is a secret to Peniel's success, it is the glorious power of Almighty God.

I want to stand on a mountaintop and cry out as loud as I possibly can: "Don't be afraid of this giant! He has already been defeated. We've got the power, and it is working in the lives of the clients at Peniel today."

Called to Pastor

I grew up in a home with good parents who took me to church. However, I began a lifestyle of partying when I was fifteen years old. A year later, I tried my first line of cocaine. By the time I was eighteen, I began my criminal career strung out on meth and crack. I started to steal and lie, doing whatever it took to support my habit. For the next several years, I was in and out of jails. At the age of twenty-four, I was facing prison time. In desperation, I cried out to Jesus, and with the help of many, God paved the way for me to end up at Peniel Ministries.

The staff at Peniel confronted me with the issues that led to my addictions. Forced to examine myself, I quickly learned that I was the problem. Peniel formed a foundation of biblical truth in me that changed my life forever. With the help of the staff of committed men and women dedicated to Christ and their tireless efforts, I completed the program in 2005.

In 2009, I became a youth pastor. Then, in 2012, I founded my own church, Life Gate Ministries. Now I am married and have four kids. Truly, I am a living example of how Peniel Ministries changes lives.—*Doug (Pennsylvania)*

CHAPTER 14

A PARENT AND A PASTOR'S WIFE

When God created Adam and Eve and placed them in the Garden of Eden, the first family was born. This family was ordained to populate and reproduce a healthy world filled with life and purpose. What we now see is the result of sin and rebellion, which has taken its toll for generations.

Christians today have a greater responsibility than ever to aid in the restoration of the family. It is possible to interrupt the dysfunction that has taken hold of our families. We must preach and teach the gospel. The multiplication of single-family homes and the changing roles of males and females continue. The drug addiction and alcoholism epidemic has disintegrated families and turned homes into war zones. In the process, it has placed our children in the high-risk category of following the same destructive path.

Can we address and correct these prevalent problems? I believe we can restore broken lives with our personal testimonies and by supporting those who are on the frontline of defense—those who are striving to connect human hands to God's hand.

From all over the United States, Canada, and other countries, clients come to a quiet town in Pennsylvania looking for treatment for drug abuse, alcoholism, sexual addiction, eating disorders, legal problems, and poverty. Their backgrounds vary, including police officers, businesspeople, parents, ministers, and other professions. Because of Peniel's high rate of success (85%) and individualized treatment, referrals come from pastors, probation officers, district attorneys, and family members.

Throughout this book, you have read testimonies of individuals whom Christ has transformed through Peniel. Now hear the testimonies of a parent and a pastor's wife.

Vicky, Parent of a 2011 Graduate

As the mother of three children, I personally know how awful it is to have a child in addiction. My youngest son started smoking weed at age twelve and quickly progressed. By the age of sixteen, he was out of control. I was distraught and unable to help him.

He stole from our home to buy drugs. He would have criminal people looking for him, having ripped them off countless times. Our family was constantly on guard. Worst of all was the horrible feeling that something devastating was going to have to happen for him to stop (death by a dealer or an overdose). At times it was comforting when he went to jail or rehab, just to know he would not be able to overdose and die. He was truly a "dead man walking," thin and frail. My son was nowhere to be found in this gray-looking corpse.

On February 10, 2010, at the age of twenty-five, he decided to go to Peniel. He was so sick of being sick and having to use heroin just to get out of bed. It was an answer to prayer! He had finally been so broken that he would allow a counselor and staff at Peniel to help him, and, most of all, give Christ an opportunity to save and deliver him from this horrid nightmare of a life of addiction.

Now celebrating four years of being addiction-free, he has joined the fight in our community toward prevention by going into schools each week to speak to students about not making the choice to try drugs. God has restored him. Our family is forever grateful to Peniel.

Pat, a Pastor's Wife

For years, the Spellmans kept telling us, "You have to come to graduation!" We were faithfully supporting Peniel with finances and prayers, but that was not enough for my friend Marion. She was unrelenting with her invitations for us to come to just one graduation. I have forgotten how many years ago when we went to our first one, but I don't think we have missed one since! Peniel's graduation is the highlight of our year.

We pastor a church and understand the joy of seeing people become overcomers and hear the amazing testimonies of broken lives being restored. We join the praise that goes up when we see and hear the amazing testimonies of broken lives being restored.

At Peniel, graduation is a weekend-long celebration of the power of God to transform lives. Each time I think, *It can't get better than this*, yet the next year is again totally amazing. We meet families of graduates and hear their stories.

During the weekend, we also hear the testimonies of the graduates themselves. We find ourselves especially listening for the ones whose families we have met that weekend. There are always comments of Peniel being a literal lifesaver. It's a place of hope after years of disappointments and despair, and a joyous celebration of shattered lives beginning anew!

As the graduates finish, they are greeted by supportive, thunderous ovations. We have never been in a place of such encouragement and support. Alumni come back to graduation year after year, as testimonies to the *keeping* power of God.

Because it is such an incredible experience, we want to share it with every member of our church. We were blessed just by participating in prayer and finances, but it wasn't until we went to graduation that we truly saw the harvest of our small contributions. I must admit, we cry abundantly at Peniel.

We are so blessed to have had God bring us in contact with the Spellmans, grow a friendship there, and allow us to pray and cheer from the sides as they and the staff carry the load. Marion was absolutely right. We *needed* to go to graduation; and since we have gone, we are committed to being there every year! We don't want to miss a single one!

Becoming a New Person

After graduating from college, I had a nice job and everything going for me. But then I decided to move to Daytona Beach, Florida, where my addiction to crack cocaine became full blown.

When I returned to my hometown in Michigan, I knew I needed help but did not know what to do. I was going to go to another program, but my pastor's daughter showed me an issue of the *Church of God Evangel,* which had an article about Peniel. The next day, I called and was accepted. When I entered the doors of Peniel, I thought I was entering treatment to beat an addiction, but I soon realized I had more than an addiction to address.

I had no integrity, character, or positive social skills. I needed to learn how to deal with adversity and pain without running to a drug or drink or attempting to kill myself. Peniel's entire program—counseling, classes, and church services—addressed these needs in my life. One of the most memorable experiences was my mother greeting me in a family session by saying, "I never thought that I would see you alive again."

Going through the program has helped me be the woman God intended for me to be. On January 4, 1999, I became part of the Peniel staff. I have served as a counselor, teacher, dorm staff, and receptionist. Currently, I am seeking to earn accreditation as a play therapist so we can also help children whose parents are caught in the web of addiction.—*Mary Jean (Michigan)*

AFTERWORD

FROM A CHAPEL TO A CHURCH

"At Last There's Hope" is boldly printed over the doors to Peniel. This is not just a catchy saying; it is the foundational truth God has used to encourage men and women who have doubted ever finding freedom from addictions.

Family members feel trapped, exhausted, and bewildered. But there is hope because of the empowering *God factor*—hope because Peniel is not just a program, it is a new way of life! It is a way of living saturated in foundational Christian principles taught and counseled from the Word of God.

From our beginning, chapel services have played an intricate role in our treatment model. In addition to learning about the wonderful things Christ has done for us, clients are able to personally experience a life-changing encounter with Him, made real by healthy Spirit-filled worship services. It is amazing how many of our clients have never been taught to respect or honor the holy things of God. We have the privilege of introducing them to the purpose and value of acknowledging and fearing Almighty God. Now they embrace the transforming results of simply believing and leaning on the beloved Son of God. Christ proves to the client that their trust in Him is the reason their inner determination, counseling sessions, and treatment plans are accomplishing the transformation that alluded them before.

We knew that regularly scheduled chapel services would also help to establish consistent church-attendance patterns in the clients' lives that would hopefully continue after completing our program. We have witnessed countless testimonies of salvation, healings, and deliverance among the clients, and even among their family members who were caught in lifetime addictions and emotional bondages. It is too late to tell me the Christian treatment model does not work. As Bishop T. D. Jakes said, "It will work, if you work it."

The early days of the Peniel Praise Chapel were a precious time of learning and growing. We will never despise our humble beginnings, because they were not humble at all—they were rich in seeing the mighty hand of God move things and people around to accomplish His will. God profoundly spoke and fulfilled His Word in those Dillsburg chapel services. The praises would echo throughout the facility, so much so it seemed nature itself had joined us in worship. In our less than seven-foot-high ceiling and with an old wood-burning stove strategically placed, we would gather to sing and study the great and wonderful things of God. The Holy Spirit would touch and deliver the clients. Men and women would see the Lord for the first time through the anointed and preached Word of God.

Our First Chapel in Dillsburg

We did not have a musician, but we had jubilant handclapping music. We did not have decorations on the walls, but His glory filled the room. We worshiped in a wooden cabin and prayed at a homemade altar. Although our crude altar did not appeal to the natural eye, the students were taught to cry out to Almighty God as they knelt there before Him. Apparently, the Lord did not care that the altar lacked worldly elegance, because He met staff and students there every time.

Those early days produced some of the most life-changing services I have ever experienced. Many of the clients who came through that era some thirty years ago are diligently serving God today, and even preaching the glorious gospel. They were birthed in the blazing fires of the Peniel morning chapel services.

Because God was there, I thought we would always be in Dillsburg. I remember telling the clients often that I did not want to be anywhere without God. So, even with the large utility bills and functioning in a less than appropriate setting, I was willing to remain and make it work. However, like the mother eagle, God used our landlord to push us out of the nest to better things.

After it was obvious we could not arrive at a meeting of the minds with our landlord, we looked for a new home. We were able to find it, even though the program had to separate into two divisions. Although it was difficult operating in two locations, our response to this adversity was to take our clients' treatment to another level. This move caused us to expand our curriculum.

Spelly approved an unconventional approach to our general treatment plans because we had so many men that obviously had a calling on their lives. Robert Cox, a staff member, had suggested we institute a public-speaking class. After several how-to sessions, Robert would have someone in the class prepare a message for a morning chapel service. That client would then be graded on preparation, presentation, and passion. Robert would also consider their personal life choices within the dorm setting. He would often tell the class it was important that they lived what they preached.

During their free time, it was not unusual to see several clients in different corners of the room with five or six study books. They would be in deep thought preparing for a chapel service they had been assigned. Chapel services were maturing the clients as it related to the spiritual component of our program. The great messages our students delivered were unbelievable!

Although it was difficult operating from two locations, the students grew by leaps and bounds. Many made life-changing decisions that propelled them into marvelous aftercare opportunities. My opinion was that even though we still did not have a church in which to worship (which I personally longed for), I decided, *Let's just make this situation work since God is in it!*

Unfortunately, it was not to be! To remain on the Sawyer Ranch and the Camp Sertoma grounds was no longer an option. The renovation costs were outrageous; it was time for us to move again.

You will remember our move to the beautiful farmhouse in York Springs. One of our first projects was to transform the cellar of a former apple-crating factory into a chapel. Here is where we had "flat-out" church. Ministers from far and near came to preach and teach our fifty clients. That little building was rockin'! In addition to having chapel in the mornings, we began evening services, and people in the community came. It was not unusual to see students and visitors alike kneeling side-by-side and weeping before the Lord.

Again, I was so sure this was our permanent home that I even chose the spot to build our long-awaited church. No longer would we have a makeshift chapel, but a genuine sanctuary for our students to worship our God in a setting He deserved. It would sit independently on the pinnacle of a hill directly above all of our day-to-day activities. Finally, we were "home"!

Then came a letter from the state's Department of Drugs and Alcohol Programs (DDAP). It was a nonnegotiable notice stating that unless we built a large dormitory, cafeteria, and proper offices within three months, we could not continue to occupy this property. Surely this was a mistake, because we had already made many changes so that the property would safely accommodate the program. After all, the Lord was guiding us and had already given us the land. But the DDAP did not see it that way—and, once again, we found ourselves homeless.

At that time, Bishop Garland Griffis was our Church of God state overseer. He heard of the dilemma we were facing and he refused to see this ministry interrupted. He invited us to move onto the state campgrounds, releasing the buildings that were not being occupied.

Those days were difficult but full of promise. As a part of the agreement, Peniel was responsible for maintaining the grounds, which were extensive. We had to reschedule classes and counseling sessions. It was a challenge, but we were up to the task. This new home presented great growth opportunities.

Not everyone was pleased with Bishop Griffis' decision. We found out later that he withstood painful disapproval and sharp criticism. Still, he stood steadfast and unmovable. God was leading him and he had the courage to follow. Who would ever guess that as I write this book, his son, Dr. David Griffis, is the Peniel liaison to the Church of God Executive Committee! He represents Peniel to the international church leadership.

After the term of Garland Griffis expired, the leadership was transferred to Bishop W. A. Davis. Meanwhile, the ministers across the state were considering if retaining the campgrounds was prudent.

COG Campgrounds—Somerset

Peniel had settled in to do the work of God on that property in Somerset. God had given us the location, so I was not overly concerned about the campground being sold. The ministers had been talking about selling it for as long as I could remember. So, I figured it was just talk—nothing would come of it!

We were worshiping in the large cafeteria and God was blessing. People were attending our services from the community, so much so that Bishop Davis would tease Spelly. He told him he needed to organize this "bootleg church." We all laughed, not knowing that God was planting the seed. It was not an official church, but God certainly was meeting with us on a regular basis. We were just thrilled to be in our home and to stabilize the program once again.

The annual state camp meetings were incredible. Our staff and clients were welcome to attend. We decided to incorporate the information from those meetings into our curriculum. The morning Bible teachers were phenomenal, always dropping precious life-changing nuggets that would inevitably confirm earlier Peniel classes or counseling sessions. And the night speakers were so anointed and so full of God's truth that our clients would speak about their messages for months. Some of the speakers would stay over just to minister exclusively to the Peniel clients after the services had concluded.

During these meetings, many of our clients were saved, some were baptized in the Holy Spirit, and others were healed. It was like a piece of heaven. All was right with the world . . . until the word came that the ministers in the state had indeed voted to sell the campground. Again, we found ourselves packing and in search of a permanent home. I can still hear Bishop Griffis teasing us about Peniel moving even more than the children of Israel, who wandered in the wilderness for forty years.

First, we had to meet with the staff and break the news that we were moving *again*. We're talking about moving a dorm full of people, clothes, furniture, appliances, office equipment, files, and boxes of documents. We also had the task of notifying people of our new address, including families, vendors, supporters, and the various medical and legal systems to which we were accountable. Then there were the grueling hours spent packing, unpacking, and setting up.

Finally, I said to Spelly, "Please just take me to the movies." I told him I wanted to see a comedy—I just needed to get away. We chose the classic *It's a Mad, Mad, Mad, Mad World.* I thought, *Well, at least the title is right*! However, the movie opened with Jimmy Durante literally dying! Hmm!

Well, the search was on—we had to find a place to go. I lived under a dark, frightening cloud until one morning Spelly came in from his daily run. Everyone knew this was when he spent his quality time with the Lord. When he came in the door, he was beside himself with excitement. Spelly does not overly express his feelings, but this day he was different.

"Babe," he said. "Sit down and listen. God has spoken to me! As sure as my name is Harold Spellman, God has spoken to me." Emphasizing the glory of it all, he said, "He gave me 2 Samuel 7:10: 'I will appoint a place for My people Israel, and will plant them, that they may dwell in a place of their own and move no more; nor shall the sons of wickedness oppress them anymore, as previously' (NKJV). Babe, trust me on this: All is well."

By this time, Bishop Danny May was the state overseer, and he was also the chairman of our board of directors. He was up to the task ahead. His business savvy and wisdom were incredible. Spelly and I met with Reverend May and a realtor at a local restaurant about the property that Spelly and Jim Osipov, a dear friend of the ministry, had located. The realtor was double-talking and began to dance around the issues. Reverend May picked up his papers, put them in his briefcase, and said, "I am so out of here."

The realtor caught us at the door and said, "Reverend May, you are masquerading as a preacher, but you are really a shrewd businessman. I am ready to deal!" Bishop May spearheaded the subsequent purchase of our Johnstown facility, which became our permanent home, just as God had said. So we moved for the last time.

Johnstown Home

Meanwhile, the community was attending our services held in our large cafeteria. After one of his visits, Overseer May approached us about organizing a church. Reverend Spellman was already preaching like his coat was on fire, and men and women were responding to his ministry. "Yes," we said, "we certainly do not want to be a maverick or a loose cannon in God's church. We want to be accountable." So Bishop May organized the Peniel Praise Chapel on July 24, 1994, with ninety-one people—later renamed the Peniel Praise Community Church.

After Reverend May's tenure, another state leadership transition took place. Bishop Rodney Jeffords was appointed as the Pennsylvania overseer. If ever God had sent a dynamic ministry team into our midst, it was Rodney and Sandra Jeffords, who came to us from Alaska.

During the first state meeting under their tenure, I got a clue of the quality of their commitment. A woman pastor from Alaska had recently relocated to Pennsylvania and was now serving at Peniel. After a morning session, Mrs. Jeffords asked to see the former pastor. She set aside all of her busyness and even dining with officials just to spend one-on-one quality time with this woman. Mrs. Jeffords wanted to see if there were any needs she might have with her move to Pennsylvania. Mrs. Jeffords was just settling in herself, but her thoughts were on one of her former pastors, and she would not rest until she knew that this woman was safely settled.

The Jeffords demonstrated the same shepherd's heart for the churches and ministries of Pennsylvania. The state Women's Board raised thousands of dollars for Peniel under Mrs. Jeffords' leadership. These monies made it possible for over sixty clients to receive treatment. Peniel was not unique in getting the Jeffords' support. If the work was of God, count them in! The Jeffords are extraordinary leaders who have a passion for the hurting, and they continue to support Peniel.

We had finally and safely moved into our "promised land." Dr. Robert Fisher became chair of our board of directors. He skillfully helped guide us through the maze that was to lead us to our dream of having a permanent home. He protected us from disgruntled "boo birds," and lovingly assisted us in obtaining finances to address overwhelming expenses.

Upon settling at 760 Cooper Avenue, our permanent home, Dr. Fisher's first goal was to repair the parking lot, which was a grand mess. He felt strongly that because it was an eyesore, the community, as well as the clients, would notice it first. He said the clients needed to come in the doors with respect for the facility. The parking lot was in such disarray that he questioned if it would have a negative effect on Peniel supporters.

Church in Johnstown

Although the repair of the parking lot was

the priority, we soon learned that a greater issue was brewing. Strong resistance from the community was making local headlines. We discovered we were being sued by the local school board, county commissioners, and the township! They were vehemently challenging our charitable organization status. The weeks that we spent in court were excruciating.

The presiding judge was the Honorable F. Joseph Leahey. It seemed like every day of the trial, a new negative report was chronicled in the local newspaper. Someone in the community accused the Spellmans of building a mansion on the Peniel property! One morning during the trial, with no prior notice, Judge Leahey adjourned the session in his courtroom to meet at our home. He walked throughout it and finally said, "This house is very nice, but it certainly is *not* a mansion."

After hearing all of the evidence, and after his careful deliberation, Judge Leahey stated we had not violated the laws and ruled in our favor. It took courage and integrity for him to make that ruling. I believe Judge Leahey was an instrument in the hands of Almighty God. God had promised Spelly that he had prepared a place for us . . . and God was faithful.

Through it all, we continued to have great services in the cafeteria. Spelly would tell the congregation the community had a right to want to feel safe, and it was our responsibility to run a tight ship to ensure their safety. He admonished us not to respond negatively.

However, his was not the only concern we were facing. Everyone at Peniel knew the Jeffords' tenure in Pennsylvania would end in 2010. We wondered, *What if the new overseer knew nothing about the work of Peniel?* The wonderful day came when the news of Dr. Ken Bell's appointment to Pennsylvania was announced. We had known and loved Ken and Tricia Bell for years!

We couldn't wait to invite Mrs. Bell to minister to our congregation. She is an educator personified and a woman with great spiritual depth. She blew us away! She gave me the notes to her message, and I fully intend to use them someday.

As a long-standing member of the board of directors, it is impossible to write about all of the problems Dr. Bell had already helped us work through. The graver the challenge, the greater his anointing! When Dr. Bell was assisting Peniel in establishing our website, the company we were using was not performing as agreed. For weeks I disputed with them, to no avail. In a phone conversation, I mentioned the problem to Dr. Bell. He was fully aware of the company's responsibilities, and he calmly said, "Marion, let me give them a call." Exactly what he said to them, I don't know, but within the hour the company called asking me what they could do to satisfy Peniel.

We have a special place in our facility where we have hung a picture of Dr. Bell. He has proven the caption on the picture is altogether fitting: "Only once in a lifetime will you have the opportunity and the honor to meet a Dr. Kenneth R. Bell."

Soon the community joined us for Sunday worship services, and the room was filled to capacity each week. Still, the finances did not match the attendance and we struggled to stay alive. We had a beautiful facility, but with that came four-figured frightening utility bills, huge insurance costs, large food bills, and so forth. However, God was with us. He was saving and healing regularly. He was blessing the people and revealing Himself in every service. Various denominations were represented in our services. People from different walks of life would attend. It was not unusual to see a church group just show up to help us in any way they could. Yet, we still did not have a church building.

Following Dr. Robert Fisher's term as chairperson of the board of directors, Dr. Gene Rice was elected. I will never forget the private meeting I had with him in our boardroom. "Miss Marion," he asked, "what is your present vision for Peniel?"

Of course, I couldn't wait to tell him! Somehow I knew he would be able to help us achieve my lifelong dream. "Dr. Rice, I want to build a real church. Even with the tremendous results we are experiencing in our chapel services, I long for an edifice that will be independent and exclusively designated for worship services. I want our clients to actually attend church . . . in a church. I don't want them confused when they leave; they must unite with a church under a pastor if they are going to be successful."

As I explained my heart, I saw it when it happened. He did not say it, but I knew he had caught my vision. It was the right time, the right place, with the right man. Dr. Gene Rice had been called by God for this particular season. He spearheaded the capital campaign to remodel the entire facility. He raised millions of designated dollars. In addition to this, he helped us build our church.

Not only do we have a beautiful edifice, we even have a smaller chapel that we have gratefully named "The Gene Rice Power Extravaganza Room." It is the least we could do for a man willing to allow God to use him to make my dream of over thirty years come true.

As I reflect on how far we have come, and how God orchestrated our moves and relocation projects, I stand in awe at the mighty hand of God on Peniel. He has taught us how to trust Him. He has proven that His word is altogether true and He will never fail us.

Students in Worship

Johnstown Construction

My sister, Lori, had to respond to a young client who declared he was going to worship Muhammad in the dorm while we attended our regularly scheduled church service. She looked him in the eyes and said, "You are free to worship anyone you choose, but you cannot do it here! Jesus Christ is Lord in this place, and we worship Him only!"

We have committed to honor God with our worship, with a good name, and with a successful program. His Spirit is always welcome, and we are committed to teach and preach the Word of God without compromise.

Like King David, whose desire was to build a permanent house of worship for the Lord, we wanted to build a place of worship for Almighty God. Moving from a chapel status to a bona fide church was not a road without bumps, bruises, and hard work; yet, it was worth every single step and every hard place. We would do it again!

> *Moreover I [God] will appoint a place for my people Israel [Peniel], and will plant them, that they may dwell in a place of their own, and move no more; neither shall the children of wickedness afflict them any more, as beforetime* (2 Sam. 7:10).

Johnstown Facility, Our Permanent Home

PENIEL TIMELINE

- February 1980: Decision made to leave Bureau of Corrections to begin developing vision of a Christian-oriented residential treatment program
- February—October 1980
  - Name chosen
  - Program designed and written
  - Articles of incorporation written
  - Bylaws established
  - Board of directors chosen
  - Staff chosen (26 responded)
  - Staff meetings held in the Spellmans' living room
- October 31, 1980: Acquired first facility—Footlight Ranch (Wellsville)
- November—December 1980: Building preparations/renovations of facilities
- December 1980—January 1981: Staff training at new facility
- January 17, 1981: Dannibelle concert at Messiah College (Harrisburg)—fundraiser for the opening of Peniel
- February 2, 1981: Received first two residents and operations officially began
- April 17, 1982: Peniel's first graduation held at Messiah College, with Reverend Ben Kinchlow from The 700 Club as keynote speaker. Reverend Kinchlow tours grounds and gives us a prophetic word during the tour to "possess the land."

- July 4, 1982: Board calls three-day fast due to conflict with property owner threatening to triple rent or evict.
- August 1982: Eviction notice given; Sheriff hangs "for sale" sign on the building.
- August 1982: Move to Mount Wolf
- September 1982: Township meeting held over ordinance violations. Lacey Hayes speaks to township group. Peniel denied a permit to operate residential treatment center at this facility unless the barn is moved.
- September 1982: God raises up a "ram in the bush" with permission to occupy Camp Sertoma facility in Linglestown (Lacey Hayes).
- December 4, 1982: Move to York Springs facility
- June 25, 1988: Move to Somerset Campgrounds
- April 1993: Purchase of Peniel's permanent home (Johnstown)
- 1993—present: "The task is impossible; therefore, let us proceed!"

ABOUT THE AUTHOR

In 1971, Marion Spellman developed a program designed to help hurting and addicted men and women in our society. Growing up, she witnessed firsthand the devastating effects of substance abuse with her own brother and the pain that it caused her family.

Dr. Spellman vowed to help, so she started a program with the desire to prevent other families from enduring the same pain her family suffered. The desire grew as she witnessed an increase in broken homes, community deterioration, and overwhelming crime. She also observed that most of the reported crimes were drug-and-alcohol related. Recidivism was the norm.

Dr. Spellman began by working with incarcerated women in the Allegheny County Jail located in west-central Pennsylvania during the early 1970s. She had a desire to see women not only free from repetitive incarceration, but also free from the cause of their addictions. There she began reasoning with individuals in the prison and witnessing dramatic and lasting success.

She gained experience in the field of drug-and-alcohol treatment in the late 1970s at a Christian drug-and-alcohol treatment facility in western Pennsylvania. After some time, she was promoted to director of the female component of the program and specialized in personal care and spiritual growth. Dr. Spellman was able to see the benefit of a structured program for individuals who had developed irresponsible living habits.

Following her tenure, she was employed at the Pennsylvania Bureau of Correction in the commissioner's office. However, her promotion to this position did not erase the desire in her heart to see lives changed, and in 1980 she founded Peniel.

Peniel was established without the benefit of start-up capital. It was birthed with a deep desire to provide effective professional rehabilitation for men and women who require long-term inpatient treatment for chronic drug and/or alcohol addiction or for mild emotional problems. The program has served thousands of men and women from nearly every state as well as foreign countries.

From its humble beginnings in Dillsburg, Peniel continues to chase its vision and maintain its standard for excellence. The physical plant was expanded to include a sanctuary, two dormitories, a full gymnasium, a weight room, learning center, a full library, a medical wing, and a family visiting area. Services have been extended to include licensed outpatient component. The credentialed staff members are committed and capable.

As Peniel has crossed the threshold of thirty successful years of effective Christian treatment, the staff enthusiastically looks forward to a bright and promising future. Men and women continue to seek help for their life-dominating addictions, and God continues to bless Peniel with the capability to serve.

PENIEL AND YOU

Peniel needs financial supporters in order to continue and flourish. When you make a tax-deductible donation to this ministry, you become a partner in rebuilding the lives of individuals who have been ravaged by chronic drug and alcohol addictions.

www.penielrehab.com
814-536-2111
Peniel
Box 250
Johnstown, PA 15907

You may also know someone who can benefit from this state-licensed Christian treatment program. Contact the Peniel offices for more information.